LOOKING TO JESUS

LOOKING TO JESUS

KESWICK MINISTRY

Michael Baughen on Hebrews
Charles Price on 1 Samuel
PLUS many other messages

Edited by David Porter

OM Publishing
PO Box 48, Bromley, Kent, England

Keswick Convention Council, England

Cover photos: The Rev. Canon K.W. Coates, BA
(Used by kind permission)

British Library Cataloguing in Publication Data

Looking to Jesus: Keswick Ministry.
1. Bible—Critical studies
I. Porter, David *1945*–
220.6

ISBN 1-85078-082-X

OM Publishing is an imprint of Send The Light
(Operation Mobilisation),
PO Box 48, Bromley, Kent, England, BR1 3JH

Production and Printing in England by
Nuprint Ltd, Station Road, Harpenden, Herts, AL5 4SE.

CONTENTS

CHAIRMAN'S INTRODUCTION

The 1990s at Keswick opened with a gentle experiment, breaking the tradition of many years. We alternated one speaker and two speakers at the evening meetings. We circulated a questionnaire to get people's reactions. Generally speaking, the experiment was well received.

Certainly the quality of the preaching remained very high and this book will reflect something of it. Cold print never easily conveys the warmth of preaching, particularly where a preacher has a relaxed conversational style. It is one of the joys of the Keswick platform that people with very different ways of preaching blend their messages together.

It is very important that there should be a continuing clarity of exposition from Scripture but it is very healthy that this should not be in a stereotyped manner. Sometimes evangelicals have erred in seeking to have a rather uniform style of preaching, which could well have restricted the Spirit and certainly would not produce the rich variety that I believe is evident in these pages.

1990 had an episcopal flavour about it. We were able to announce the appointment of George Carey as the new Archbishop of Canterbury with great joy. I wrote to him with the greetings of the Keswick Convention and received back a very warm personal letter in which he informed me that in their early days he and his wife had benefited much from the ministry of Keswick and were sorry that recently they had not been able to return. Perhaps one day we shall have an archbishop on the platform!

But we profited enormously this year from the Bible Readings from Hebrews of Michael Baughen, the Bishop of Chester. These studies demonstrate the possibility of doing a verse-by-verse exposition of a whole book in four mornings. We were certainly kept moving but without a sense of unholy rush.

The theme of those Readings took us very much to the centrality of the person of Jesus. The modern hymn *Name of All Majesty* was the theme that ran through the Bible Readings, and a Convention can do nothing better than major on the wonder of who Jesus was and is. The letter to the Hebrews takes us beyond the work He accomplished once for all at Calvary into the glory of His ascension and victory.

To follow through these studies again by using this book, or tape and video, would only enrich all of us. I felt guided by the Lord to start the whole Convention with words from Hebrews 12, again focusing away from ourselves to Jesus. By the grace of God the whole Convention took on that theme of the encouragement of the triumph of Jesus.

During the Holiday Convention Charles Price, one of the youngest men to take the Bible Readings at the Convention in recent years, with a very different style from Michael Baughen, led us through some very relevant chapters in 1 Samuel.

I am constantly amazed at how contemporary the Old Testament is and we were faced with some searching challenges about our choices. All too often we opt for ritual rather than reality. The final Bible Reading of the Holiday Convention included a very moving appeal to personal commitment from Charles Price; a considerable number of people felt guided to make that response public.

This fits with the whole ethos of the 1990 Convention. There were more people professing conversion than I can remember for a long time and although the numbers making open commitment at the World View meeting may not have been as large as sometimes, there was a very real sense of dedication and commitment. Both the World View meetings put the challenge to service in a very demanding way. I believe it is vital that we ask people to make a commitment which is sacrificial after the pattern of Scripture.

Once more we can rejoice that the Keswick Convention was blessed with remarkably good weather. Perhaps this helped to create an atmosphere of gratitude and joyfulness. Most of us who are by now regulars at Keswick agreed that it was one of the happiest Conventions we can remember.

The joy of the modern media is that the ministry can continue. I trust these pages will be part of that continuing ministry, encouraging those of us who come regularly to the Convention to keep faithful, reminding others of the value of a whole week under the authority of God's word and challenging us all to keep looking to Jesus.

Philip Hacking
Chairman of the Keswick Convention Council

EDITOR'S INTRODUCTION

Editing the annual Keswick volume is in some ways an odd experience. The aim is to preserve as much as possible of the unique Keswick atmosphere, while at the same time including all the teaching in the selected talks and addresses. In addition, we plan to produce the finished book, edited, typeset, printed, bound and in the shops all in good time for Christmas; and we take care that the book does not end up so weighty a volume that its price becomes too high. To achieve this, the staff of Send The Light work wonders to provide transcripts of the taped addresses, and as editor I wield my electronic scissors and abridge the text by up to fifty per cent on my word processor.

My only defence as I cut and trim is that I take no pleasure in my task. Many of the illustrations, jokes, anecdotes and amplifications that I have cut from this year's material were helpful, challenging and sometimes simply entertaining to me personally. I am no thoughtless vandal slashing left and right regardless. After thirteen years as editor, the choices get no easier.

Those of you who were privileged to be at the Convention and remember the material that had to be left out are reminded of the excellent tape and video library (details on p. 253). In the meantime, you hold in your hands a record of the eight Bible Readings and a selection of the addresses, edited to preserve all the teaching and much of the flavour of the event.

New readers should be aware that the speakers have very little time to check the edited material; this is a record of a spoken occasion, not a book written by its authors for print from the outset and revised through several drafts.

Bible quotations have been checked against the relevant version, except where the speaker was obviously paraphrasing. As the speakers themselves frequently remind us, a Bible kept open by your side as you read will greatly enhance your enjoyment and understanding.

David Porter
Editor

THE BIBLE READINGS

Jesus—Name of All Majesty

by Bishop Michael Baughen

1. We See Jesus—Who He Is (Hebrews 1–2)

You may think that trying to do the whole of Hebrews in four mornings is a tall order. If so, you're quite correct! But we're going to go through some of the most magnificent scenery in the New Testament. And I hope, by God's grace, that it will prove so for many of us, as we work through this book together.

Background

Why Hebrews?

Some of the major issues facing us in our country and in the Christian church today are addressed by this book. Let me tell you what some of them are.

There is a tremendous attack being made at present upon *the person of Jesus Christ*. The denigration of Jesus as the Son of God is subtly going on both outside and inside the church. We must stand firm on this issue and know our ground. People like Don Cupitt have said publicly that it is now not necessary to believe that Jesus is divine; for some reason he's still allowed to keep his Orders in the Church of England.

There are attacks upon *the atonement*. Many people

regard any idea of Christ dying in our place upon the cross as abhorrent and irrelevant. To them, the cross has become an example, a wonderful thing but certainly not an atonement.

There are those who attack *the Scriptures* as God's truth revealed. They actually say—as I heard someone say the other day—that there are just a few stepping-stones of reliability within the New Testament. Or, as I heard someone else say, that there is nothing certain whatsoever in the New Testament.

There are those who attack *the concept of eternal life*. Believe it or not, there are actually theologians who no longer believe there is any life after death.

There are those who attack *the holiness of Christian living*, and not least the stand we take on Christian morality.

There are those who attack *the Christian faith* so that they actually believe we should go back towards Judaism; and there are those who feel that we should therefore not seek in any way to evangelise Jews.

And there's a weakening in the commitment of many Christian people to be prepared to suffer for Jesus Christ; they want a life of cream cakes and nothing else.

All these issues are encountered in the Epistle to the Hebrews. That is why I believe it is one of the most important epistles for the Christian church to grasp at the present time.

Alongside all this is the influence of the New Age Movement which is growing fast and subtly, because it answers to the human spirit without God. It's the oldest form of spiritist religion, but now has all the power of the media behind it. It expects Christianity, Judaism, and Islam to be eliminated: there is no God out there, only within you. The New Age Movement, whose books and literature are being consumed in vast quantities across this

land and across this world, stands against Jesus Christ as
the Son of God and the Saviour of the world.

The book of Hebrews was particularly written to converted Jews who felt drawn back to Judaism. They were
pulling out of the assembly (chapter 10). They were not
obeying their leaders (chapter 13).

We don't know who wrote it. Nothing in the epistle
points to Paul, and Timothy is referred to as 'our brother',
which Paul would never say. But that's just precisely what
Hebrews is about; it denigrates the author, because Christ
is the centre of this epistle. And that is what the author
wants to communicate.

His argument is that the law and ceremonial that were
so important to Jews have been all fulfilled in Jesus Christ.
Christ is supreme in the church and in the world.

We see Jesus—who He is

The start of this epistle is like an overture; a full orchestra
in full strength playing the tremendous themes that will
emerge in different ways throughout the whole epistle.
We begin in a grand and majestic style. In three of the
most wonderful verses in the whole Bible we have one of
the most thrilling perceptions of who Jesus Christ is.

The author's concern is to get straight to Christ. Notice,
he doesn't bother with any personal greeting. He goes
right to Christ at the outset, this man who has a passion
about Christ.

Chapter 1: who is He?

1. He is the Word of God (verses 1–2)
You and I can only know another person's mind if they
tell us what is in it. We find out about people by asking
them questions. It is impossible for any human being to

know about the living God unless He reveals His mind to us. All human attempts to reach up towards God will only be partial and ineffective. God has to reveal Himself to us.

And He has spoken to us; 'to our forefathers through the prophets and at many times and in various ways, but in these last days he has spoken to us by his Son'. Before Jesus, He spoke in creation and through history, in many ways; psalms, poetry, history, prophecy and story. Yet when Jesus sits upon the throne they all recede into second place. And all that conglomeration of style and background and history fits together in the supreme, wonderful and glorious person of the Son of God, Jesus Christ. The whole Old Testament revelation points to Him.

Now here He comes into centre stage directly, personally, authoritatively—because of who He is. He is the supreme communication, the Word of the living God. He is the *logos*. 'He who hears me', He said, 'hears the Father.' So, in a hushed whisper, and yet with a triumphant thumping of the heart, we read those words: 'God has spoken to us by his Son.'

It is important to grasp that this was not a stage on the road. He was the finale. 'In these last days'—the last days began with Jesus Christ. He was the climax of the Old Testament revelation, which was progressive towards Him. There is no longer a progression that leaves Him behind. He is the initiator, the form, the basis, the rock of the New Testament revelation. It points towards Him up to His coming; it points from Him and outwards from Him, expounding Him—showing Him—revealing Him—until the end of time.

These are the last days, says Hebrews 1. Jesus began the final era. The Holy Spirit applies and teaches, but never alters, what God has said by His Son. John 16:14— 'He will glorify me, for he will take what is mine and declare it to you.'

2. He is Heir of all things (verse 2)

Notice the word 'appointed'. It's planned. There can be no equal prophet, for Jesus is appointed by God as Heir of all. You can't get more than that. There is no one else in the picture.

Paul expresses it in Ephesians: 'Far above all rule and authority and power and dominion, above every name that is named, not only in this age but in the age to come. He has put all things under his feet'—God's plan to unite all things in Him, 'things in heaven and things on earth'. Long before, the psalmist wrote: 'I have set my king on my holy hill. You are my Son. Serve the Lord with fear; with trembling. Kiss his feet.'

Christ is King. Christ is the Heir of all things. All else recedes to the steps of the throne before Him.

3. He is the Agent of creation (verse 2)

God created the world, but the Father created through Jesus, the Son. John 1: 'By him all things were made and without him was not anything made that was made.'

Christ the Agent of creation speaks to us of His eternal being. 'Before Abraham, I *Am*'; 'the glory which I had with you before the world was made'. In the incarnation, then, we believe that God did not simply enter into a man, but *became* man. He did not choose a human and make him His son, as the Jehovah's Witnesses claim. This is the incarnate, living, eternal, pre-existent Son of God who entered into the world and who was involved in the very creation of this marvellous universe.

In verse 10 we are also told that this whole creation is in the hands of God. Notice 'In the beginning' He 'laid the foundations of the earth'—that is, the foundations from which the earth developed. In Genesis 1 the word 'creation' (*bara*) is used only of the earth and heavens, life beginning in the waters, and man. God then said, 'Develop and multiply.' There is often much confusion between the fact that God is responsible ultimately for the creation, and its development. There's no confusion in Scripture; it's only in some modern people's minds.

'The heavens are the work of your hands,' says verse 10, and verse 12 speaks of the way in which He will roll them up like a robe. The end is in His control. Human beings will only destroy the world if God allows it, just as He allowed someone to crucify Jesus on the cross, only in the execution of His will. When Christians panic about what's going to happen to the world, they have forgotten that God is in control. He is the Lord of all creation. It says so plainly; 'He will roll them up like a garment', like an untidy teenager throwing a shirt into the corner (though I'm not comparing God to an untidy teenager!). He will say, 'Well, that's the end of the world. Now we'll get on with the family gathered in heaven.' That's the end; when God says so.

4. He is the Outshining of God (verse 3)

He's the Outshining—the Radiance, as the NIV puts it. The RSV says 'he reflects the glory of God', the NIV says 'the Son is the radiance of God's glory'. Does this make Him less than God? Can we look at a light bulb? You'd get spots before your eyes if you tried to look at the lights in this tent. It's dazzling to look into the light, but the effect of the light—when we see what it's doing—is marvellous.

You cannot look into the light of God—but you see the illumination flooded into the world by Jesus Christ. He is the Outshining. He is the Radiance. But there's no difference between the light that is in a light-bulb and the light that it casts on the pages of a book. It's the same light.

Jesus *is* the Light of the world, the Light of God. He is not something separate from it. That is why this term 'the Radiance', or 'the Outshining', is important. In the Old

Testament they were afraid to look upon the Shekinah glory of God. When Isaiah saw God in His majesty he said, 'I am lost; for my eyes have seen the King, the Lord of hosts.' This light needs to be mediated to us, so that we may see the wonder of God. We cannot gaze on Him, but He illuminates His truth to us in Jesus and by His Spirit. So John 1 says, 'The Light shines in the darkness and the darkness has not overcome it. The Word became flesh and we have beheld his glory, the glory as of the only Son from the Father.'

I hope that in your denomination you say the creeds. They're very important today. They're an anchor of the faith, and we need these anchors. In the Nicene Creed it says of Jesus 'He is God of God, Light of Light, Very God of Very God'. In the original it's *ek*, 'out of'. He is 'Light out of Light, Very God out of Very God'. It's an important point, not least when talking to Jehovah's Witnesses but also with many other people today on the fringes who want to reduce Jesus to a demigod.

Here, as Christ shines, we're able to see the model of how to live, and in our own lives to respond to that light and live by it; to know when we fall short of the glory of God in Romans 3, to bring others to the light, to reflect it. 'We beholding the glory of the Lord,' says Paul, 'are being changed into his glory from one degree of glory to another.' You need to be bathed in the light of Christ.

5. He is the exact representation of His being (verse 3)

'The very stamp of his nature', says the RSV. Light illuminates generally, and we might not associate it with detail. So we find an immediate corollary: 'Yes, light illuminates and it is general, but He is also the exact representation.' The Greek word used means 'character'.

I left school at fifteen and worked in an accountant's office and then as a junior in Martin's Bank. We had an electric sealing wax tool which was very modern for those days. You melted the wax with it and then pressed the Martin's Bank stamp into the wax. And there it was; the exact character. 'You can think in general about light,' says the writer, 'but now, realise that He is the *exact*, not approximate, representation of God.'

But He is, it says here, of one being with the Father. 'Being of one substance with the Father' says the Creed again. He is the very substance of God. So our response to agnostics and others who say man can never know God is that this is precisely why Christ came, so that we could know God exactly.

6. *He is the Sustainer (verse 3)*

The word used for 'sustain'—*phero*—is a very ordinary one; seeds growing, fruit bearing. It's used in Mark 2 of the four men who brought their friend to Jesus and ripped out the roof. They lowered him, you remember, to the feet of Jesus. *Phero*; they carried him to the feet of Jesus.

What stops the world flying off its axis, an octillion of stars falling, universal chaos? Scientific laws can only observe, they cannot control. The only reason it does not happen is God. He is the Sustainer. He set the world up and sustains it. When He takes His hand away, it will end, possibly with chaos at the same time as the triumph, when 'the heavens will pass away with a loud noise', says Peter, 'and the elements will be dissolved with fire, and the earth and the works that are upon it will be burned up' (2 Peter 3:10). Why? Because the day of the Lord will have come. But until then He *pheros* it; He sustains it.

And why is the world, in spite of its growth in population, still able, at least in theory, to avoid total starvation? There is enough food for the world. It's man's sin that's often prevented it. What daring, to actually write these words thousands of years ago: 'While the earth remains, seedtime and harvest, cold and heat, summer and winter,

day and night, shall not cease.' How could you dare say
that, unless you knew it was of God?

God is the Sustainer, the fruit-bearer. We thank Him
for food. However much we work and plan to provide it, it
is God who is the Sustainer. As the young child said so
wonderfully at the end of a prayer: 'Dear God, by the
way, do look after Yourself, for if anything happens to
You, we're done for!'

7. He is the Redeemer (verse 3)

'Purification for sins.' The opening overture has concen-
trated up to now on who Jesus is, just as do the first halves
of Mark, Matthew and Luke. Until you know who He is,
you're not able to hear what He's done for you. Evangelism these days needs to concentrate more exactly on what
the Gospels demonstrate: to argue who He is, because
until you know who He is, you won't hear Him. When you
know who He is, you'll begin to listen to what He's done.

Here we concentrate on who He is. We just quickly
refer to redemption, which we shall come back to in a
mighty way. It's introduced simply here with the words
'the purification for sins'—the cross, and the finished
work—'and he sat down'.

We shall come back to it; we shan't spend time now.

8. He is Lord (verses 4–14)

The writer quickly returns to his primary opening theme.
From here to the end of chapter 1 he develops the lordship
of Christ.

Look at verse 3: 'He sat down at the right hand of the
Majesty in heaven.' Verse 4: He has that name, which we
know from Philippians to be 'the name above every
name'; the name of all Majesty. And—verse 4 onwards—
He is superior to angels.

The Jews of that time had a tremendously developed
angelology. They believed in millions of angels, one for

every blade of grass in the world. Unfortunately, many Christians today tend to believe more in the devil than in angels. Yet there's as much about angels in the New Testament.

Why is He superior to them? No angel (verse 5) is called God's son. Verse 6: angels are actually going to worship Christ. Verse 7: angels have an important task, but the Son of God is King. Verse 13: angels are not over all; Christ is supreme, even over His enemies. And then the quotation from Psalm 110, the most quoted and alluded-to psalm in the New Testament. Verse 14: the angels are servants and ministers of the Saviour to serve us. We shall be surprised when we get to heaven to realise how they've been with us and helping us. Remember how they came and ministered to Jesus in the wilderness.

There's a great deal about angels here, but the important point being driven home is that Jesus is not an angel. He's not, as some of the heresies of the day argued, an angel-link in the chain between God and man. He is the Lord. He is superior to angels. He is, verse 11, the unchanging Lord of earth and heaven: 'They will be changed. But you remain the same, and your years will never end.' As Henry Lyte put it,

> Change and decay in all around I see:
> O Thou who changest not, abide with me.

Chapter 2: four things to notice

The RSV opens this chapter with 'therefore'. Unfortunately, the NIV doesn't! But it ought to, because here we come to respond to that great opening overture. And we begin to introduce other melodies, adequately expressed here, but to be enlarged later in the letter.

1. Care (verses 1–4)

We wrestle today not so much with antagonism but with sheer apathy and ignorance about Jesus Christ and His word. To most people in our country, they seem entirely irrelevant.

The writer expresses a characteristically deep concern that we should not drift away. This is not just a warning to non-Christians; it's a warning to Christians who may say 'Amen' and then not take Christ or His word seriously.

The word used means 'allowing a ship to drift through carelessness', as happened in the terrible oil slicks at sea we've heard about. The writer says that it's not so much that many Christians do this deliberately, it's just that they're careless and drift away from their earlier enthusiasm for the word. They are not anchored properly, and they drift on to the rocks.

But no message is so vital to humanity as the word of the Son of God—to Christians, above all else. At present we are urging our country and world to a decade of evangelism. It is an urgent matter, because we face a people who are allergic to God.

The old preaching of hell fire is perhaps little mentioned nowadays, yet faithful preaching of the gospel has to present both sides. So we find in verse 2 a balance between the saving message and the message of judgement. We need both together. Dangling people over the pit, producing converts by fear, is not the best way of converting anybody; because you then have to keep them by fear. On the other hand, we need to present Jesus Christ as both the Saviour of the world and the Judge of the world. The cross only has meaning against the backcloth of judgement.

How can we get people—including even Christians who grow careless—not to drift? Verse 1: 'We must pay more careful attention.' Again, it's a nautical phrase, used of mooring a ship. Our minds need to be hooked up to God's word, anchored to it in Christ, around the bollard of the word, so that no one can break that rope.

It means paying careful attention, stopping to think and examine. A large amount of evangelism today is not going to be by shouting slogans in the street. It's going to be by sitting down with people. In our ministry in London we formed an 'Agnostics Anonymous' to which many people came. There they didn't have the 'clap-trap' of the church and its services, but were able to sit, no holds barred, with other people who called themselves agnostics, who expected to destroy Christianity in three weeks; and they found the rag-bag of what they called Christianity destroyed by the truth. Yet they came. Often in London I've met people week after week by appointment, as we worked through the truth. Evangelism needs 'to reason and bring people through'. It means using books and booklets and videos and tapes, and time—to help individuals in the care and love of God.

But for us also it means discipline and an attention to how we read the Scriptures and how we use them in our evangelism. We need to ask one another to be careful with the word; it is not *a* word for mankind, it is *the* word for mankind.

Verses 3–4: It is *the* word, 'announced [past tense] by the Lord', 'confirmed' by eye-witnesses, 'testified to...by signs'—apostolic signs; the sign of a true apostle, said Paul, was signs and wonders and mighty works. What more could God do to validate His word?

To neglect it, therefore, is to neglect the greatest efforts of the living God to communicate to man, and all He has done so marvellously for the salvation of mankind.

Of course, there will be different attitudes to the Bible and to evangelism. Those who are universalists, as I fear many in the church now are, believing that everybody goes to heaven, won't be worried by neglect of the Bible. But if you believe that the gospel is a matter of life and death, you will be desperately concerned about communicating the truth, and people coming to face up to it and not to drift past it.

Take care, my brothers and sisters, how you handle the word. Don't grow careless. How many of you actually live into the word day by day, or at least week by week, with care and attention? And how many of you have grown careless? Can you face God about that, when He's given you His living word?

You've drifted. Get back! Make a determination as you walk the hills this afternoon, or in the quiet, to re-fix yourself to the bollard of the word, and not to be a drifter.

2. Contrast (verses 5–13)

The author is riveted by the paradox of the Lord of glory, the Lord of all, coming amongst us, sharing our humanity, our suffering and (verse 9) tasting death for everyone. Verses 5–8, quoting from Psalm 8, describe the special position of man in God's universe. He has often failed this trust. But Jesus is the perfect man as God intended.

Paul is equally riveted, in Philippians 2: 'Though he was in the form of God, he emptied himself and took the form of a servant'—and went to death, even the death of the cross.

My brothers and sisters, we should constantly be riveted by the sheer wonder of this contrast. The Lord of glory shared our humanity and was crucified for us. And we're to reflect this contrast in our own Christian lives.

The book of Revelation, chapter 7 (verses 13–14), says: 'Who are these clothed in white robes?...These are they who have come out of the great tribulation; they have washed their robes and made them white in the blood of the Lamb.' The history of the church is one of martyrdom, of courage. People like Stephen and Peter and Paul; missionaries going out into areas where they knew they would die. Men of courage like Archbishop Janani Luwum, shot dead by Idi Amin, like Bishop Reginald Heber, the first bishop to the whole of India who said when he arrived in India, in his late thirties, 'No man coming here can expect to live long, and will have to leave his wife and children to the care of Him who cares for the ravens.'

These are people who knew the contrast between the glory of the gospel and the readiness to be sacrificed for Jesus Christ. And we need together to be prepared to handle both the glory and the suffering of following Jesus Christ.

'It was fitting', says verse 10. He walked the path with us, for us, like us; mockery, arrest, false trial, the thirty-nine stripes, the crucifixion. What does it mean, that this made Him 'perfect'? Wasn't He perfect already? Yes, of course! It means 'complete'. As Dr Leon Morris has put it, 'Suffering introduces a perfection of testedness.' In Romans 5 it says of us that suffering produces endurance, and endurance produces character.

We are one family, and here in the contrast between Him who makes people holy and those who are made holy, He calls them brothers. The height and the depth are conflated in the person of our Lord and in the sharing of His family.

It is all to 'bring many sons to glory'. The word here means someone pioneering the way, someone throwing the line from the wrecked ship to the land over which people will go; someone blazing the path through the jungle, the founder of the firm, the organisation, the family, the town. Jesus is that; the *archegos*, who brings many sons to glory. Not to some faceless empty nirvana where one ceases to exist, but to glory, and all the fulfilment of being in the family of God.

3. Conquest (verses 14–15)

Most people, whatever they may say, are afraid of death. Many will say to you, 'Well, it's nothing, you know, I just go out like a light; there's nothing after death.' Underneath they don't believe that. People try to bury the thought of death under everything else; 'Eat, drink and be merry, for tomorrow we die.' Of course, we try to ease matters. I understand that twenty-four hour canned music is piped to embalmed bodies in some American mortuaries. Humanism has no answer to death. Everybody is going to die. But the Christian can look death in the eye—can't you?

Now, verse 15. This is part of why He came: 'He came to deliver all those who all their lives were held in slavery by the fear of death.' Of course, we can think of 'the plight of the heathen', but it's also true in Britain for millions of people. And the way in which you are delivered is not by ignoring death, not trying to push it on one side, not trying to believe it's not going to happen, but by facing it.

That is liberation theology of the best kind! You are liberated from the fear of death by the resurrection of Jesus Christ. And in that act of conquest and resurrection He made the devil ineffective—that's the word here. Death, where is your sting?

It can only be effective for us when we repent, when we lay hold of Jesus as Saviour, and His death and resurrection, when we cease to have confidence in ourselves and enter into the liberty of the children of God, His for ever.

There's a lovely moment in the communion service which many of us share, when we say, 'The bread of God keep you in *eternal life*.' You've begun it! What joy it brings!

Of course we're concerned with this life, not just with the life to come. But that shouldn't stop us witnessing to the fact that Christ has removed the sting of death for all who believe in Him. Don't be afraid of it, when people say, 'You Christians are always thinking about the next life, not about this one!' Turn their mockery against them: 'We think a lot about this life, but do you ever think about the next one?' This is the triumph, that 'nothing can separate us from the love of God in Christ Jesus'; no tribulation, pain, distress, things to come, things present. It's a wonderful truth that we have. The hope of Jesus Christ.

4. Compassion (verses 16–18)
His concern is with humankind, Abraham's descendants, and not with angels. Hence He is come to give Himself as the atonement—a wonderful word—propitiation for our sins; the sins laid not on another but on Himself.

Many people get very angry today about the idea of Jesus being the propitiation for our sins and bearing the wrath of God. They say that is barbaric. It is not barbaric when you do it to yourself. When you take on yourself the sins of the world, as God has done, then it is love to the uttermost.

This is the atonement—and we shall come back to it later. But the wonder of what emerges here at the end of chapter 2 is that our God is not some distant God; He was born and grew, and was hungry and tired, and lived and laughed and cried and suffered and died. He is our God!

Verse 18 says, 'He was tempted and suffered.' Tempted? Was it easier for Him to resist temptation as the perfect Son of God? No. I think it was the very opposite, because He saw evil for what it is; He wasn't confused like we are. He endured temptation; He endured suffering.

And the force of all this (verse 17) is that this makes Him a merciful and faithful High Priest. 'He was made like his brothers in every way, in order that he might become' that; to share with us, yes, in His death for the atonement, but to share with us as a God who can help, understand, share and come alongside us in all the sufferings of walking for Him in this world.

Care—contrast—conquest—compassion.

Take heart afresh, my brothers and sisters, in all the changes and chances of this world, all the ups and downs of church life, all the pains and joys of daily life, all the media hype, criticism and misrepresentation of the Christian church. In the midst of all this, you belong to Jesus Christ as your Saviour and Lord, and you are His for ever! For He is eternally Saviour, eternally King, eternally Lord—and no force, no heresy can alter that fact.

So have confidence, not in yourself but in Him who is the Son of God, the Word of God, the Heir of all, the Outshining, the Creator, the Exact Image, the Sustainer, the Redeemer, the Lord, the Friend and Brother. And bow before Him, Jesus, who bears the name of all Majesty.

2. Fix Your Thoughts on Jesus —How We Respond (Hebrews 3–6)

Yesterday we looked at Christ. Now we respond; today is about us. It's quite realistic and sometimes quite uncomfortable; but this is the truth of Scripture, and this is the rhythm of Hebrews.

The key word: faithful (3:2)

The word 'faithful' is the key word to this whole passage, the principal melody that runs across these next chapters. It is the mark of Jesus, who is faithful. 'Faithfulness' is one of the great descriptions of God towards us, and it's one of the great descriptions of all those who are in Christ.

I don't need to remind you that Paul speaks in Ephesians of 'those who are faithful in Christ Jesus'. Our Lord in His parable of the talents speaks of the faithful and wise servants. Revelation 2 challenges us to 'be faithful unto death and I will give you the crown of life'. All who serve Him are challenged, that it is required that those who have been given a trust must prove faithful. And later on, we shall come to Hebrews 11 with that great catalogue of those who live by faith, who are faithful in all the different circumstances of life.

Today we begin looking at Christ as faithful. Then there is a digression from 3:7 to 4:13 on *un*faithfulness. And 4:14 returns us as if there hasn't been a pause. The 'therefore' actually continues from 3:16. That's the pattern: we're going to look at faithfulness, we're going to be a bit depressed by unfaithfulness, and then we'll cheer up at the end as we come back to faithfulness.

The pattern of faithfulness (3:1–6)

Moses

Supremely, we 'fix our eyes upon Jesus' as our pattern. But we're also (verse 2) to consider Moses as a pattern of faithfulness. Verse 5 tells us that 'Moses was faithful as a servant in all God's house'.

Moses is one of my heroes. When I was made an incumbent at Manchester, I had been previously invited to take two Bible readings for the Oxford Christian Union. They had asked for two Bible studies on Moses. At that time, taking up a new parish, there were many pressures upon me, and I considered withdrawing; but in the end I felt I had to do what they'd asked.

It transformed my ministry. As I studied Moses afresh I found him to be such a real person; his humanity, his crying out to God, his frustration with some of the problems that surrounded him. Good preparation for being a bishop!

Moses had to face all that. And yet, his courage! Facing Pharaoh, the Red Sea, coming down from the mountain when they'd all gone berserk over the molten calf...I had to ask myself, do I believe in the same God? And if I do believe that the God of Moses is the God of today, then I can face anything that God calls me to do. It is the same God who pushed back the waters of the Red Sea and fed His people in the wilderness.

If there is something that distinguishes Moses, it is that

almost to the end he had a 'stickability'. He kept on and kept on, all the way through. And this is something that we ourselves are called to be—to be faithful in God's house, in whatever task we're called to.

People often say to me, 'Do you enjoy being a bishop?' And my answer is, 'Sometimes!' I didn't choose the job. There are many places, if I am honest, in which I would rather be. But the place we most want to be is where God has called us to be. And if this is that job, with all the brickbats and misunderstanding and yet all the opportunities and joys, then this is the place that I am to be— worked out before God and faithful.

And this is true whatever our task, my brothers and sisters. It's very easy to look over the fence and say, 'If only I were So-and-so. If only I weren't this. If only this hadn't happened to me. If only I were that!' But God has called you where you are, and it is there He wants you to be faithful.

This is the mark of Moses. He wouldn't have chosen that life; he had a pretty comfortable one before. But God called him to it, and he stands out through the whole of the Old Testament as the supreme example of faithfulness.

Christ more than Moses

Christ is also a faithful servant (verse 2) to the one who appointed Him. But Christ is more than that. He is also faithful as a Son over God's house (verse 6). To the Jews to whom this letter was particularly written, there was no one who had ever walked closer to God than Moses. The writer says, 'Yes, there is! It is Jesus!' Moses, he says, was part of the house of God. Christ was over it. Christ is the builder of it, and therefore worthy of greater honour.

It is important to grasp that you and I are both sons and servants. One night in London, at All Souls, Langham

Place, I preached on Paul as the slave of Christ. Afterwards someone bore down on me in the church porch; the
first person out. He grabbed me by the lapels and said: 'I
will not be called a slave of Jesus Christ. I'm a son, by the
grace of God.' He was very angry.

So then I caught hold of *him* by the lapels and said,
'Let's just try and sort this out. I'm a son saved by the free
grace of Christ. But in Romans that comes after all the
explanation of the gospel—"I appeal to you to present
your bodies as a living sacrifice." God doesn't *compel* you
to be a servant; He *asks* you to be a servant: but you have
to take it on. You are a son by grace; you are a servant by
volunteering. But once you have become a servant then
you put yourself under the command of Christ. That's
when you begin to call Him Lord and not just Saviour.'

I don't know whether he understood it, but you and I
are both sons and servants. So we share the wonderful
privilege of being members of the eternal family, as 'holy
brothers share in the heavenly calling'. And that is something important to us. We're His children by grace. But
we are also to be faithful to Him as His servants, if we've
taken that on; in the task to which He's called us, which
He has given us to do for Him. The two themes come
together here, and we have this mark of faithfulness: to be
as sons and servants.

Well, that's a wonderful start, because we've been
looking at Jesus.

The path of unfaithfulness (3:7–4:13)

Now we come to the path of unfaithfulness, and we look
at this in 3:7 to 4:13. First, the *path of unfaithfulness*, and
then the *prevention of unfaithfulness*.

Take care, says 4:1: 'Since the promise of entering his
rest still stands, let us be careful that none of you be found
to have fallen short of it.'

The warnings that come here are the warnings about complacency. You and I believe in the preservation of the saints. But once you become complacent, be very careful! God is saying here, 'Yes, there's a great truth, but be careful.' Don't be complacent: there, but for the grace of God, go I.

Perhaps you came suddenly to Christ, in a dramatic moment—the joy of coming to know Him, the exciting discoveries in the faith, in the word, in Christ, in Christian fellowship. Every Sunday you couldn't wait for the next Sunday to come...Was it like that for many of you? The earnest desire to follow and to grow and to serve? Yet, as the parable of the sower warns so clearly, we can receive the word with joy, and believe for a while, but in time of temptation fall away. Or again, we can believe and yet are choked by the cares and riches and pleasures of life, and our fruit does not mature.

There are many warnings in Scripture not to be complacent. We are to be good ground, where the word falls in and brings forth fruit. The joyful honeymoon of our faith is often revived—the wonderful moments in worship when you feel, 'A little nudge and I'd be in heaven!' It's awful to have to come back to earth. But that's God's grace, isn't it? The moments of resuscitation, when we have the renewal of the honeymoon, the wonder. Yet we cannot live in a permanent high. We have to live in the valley for Christ. And the Christian life has to develop in steadfastness and service.

So, brothers and sisters, learn to discern the symptoms of falling away.

The progression
Notice how it can often progress. Remember Psalm 1: 'Blessed is the man who does not walk in the counsel of the wicked or stand in the way of sinners or sit in the seat of mockers.' You begin by just going along with them,

then you start to identify with them, and then you are committed to them and so you start mocking the position you were once in. That is the warning of Psalm 1. It's a progression. The point is, to discern when you begin to walk—before the next stages come.

1. A hardening of the heart (3:7)

In 3:7–11 there is a quotation from Psalm 95. This psalm was, for the Jews, one of the very special psalms with which to start the Sabbath—just as in the Church of England; it's in Morning Prayer.

The incident comes in the story of Moses and the exodus, and concerns lack of faith about the promised land. Joshua and Caleb believed and the rest did not, and that committed them to thirty-eight years' wandering and delay. It is quoted here as an example of people hardening their hearts: 'If you hear the word, do not harden your hearts.'

Sunday by Sunday in the Anglican liturgy you hear, 'Harden not your hearts.' It is a warning about how easy it is to do so. Jesus said Himself, 'Those who have ears to hear, let them hear.' Often people don't want to hear. He said, 'You went out to hear John the Baptist in the wilderness; what did you expect to see? And when you got out there, and he wasn't what you expected, you didn't like it.'

'He who has ears to hear, let him hear.' Do not stop, do not close your ears. 'You—' He says to the churches in the book of Revelation—'some of you are losing your first love. Some of you are bringing in false teaching. Some of you are lukewarm.'

Can you hear it? Or—because you have begun to slip—have you begun to harden your heart, so that you can ignore and pass by the word of God because you don't want to hear it? That's when you begin to harden.

How well do we hear? How well do we really come openly to the word of God? How easily we harden our hearts to it!

2. A turning away (3:12)

The consequences of hardening our heart is that we then turn away from the living God. We develop (verse 12) 'a sinful, unbelieving heart'.

It is this progression that begins to be able to avoid the truth, as our parents did in the garden of Eden—to try to live without Him as if He doesn't exist. And if we don't want to hear Him, we soon don't want to have contact with Him. We soon stop reading the word, we begin to be careless about worship, or the membership of the fellowship, the house group, or the Bible study group. Eventually, perhaps, we don't go to church at all. Our turning away progresses because we do not want to be convicted by the word. Therefore we avoid it.

In 3:16–18, he quotes Israel's rapid slipping away. And what an incredible slipping it was! Moses was delayed on the top of the mountain over the giving of the Ten Commandments; and there followed the extraordinary incident of the molten calf and the sexual orgy that accompanied it. So quickly! And when Aaron is called to give account, he makes one of the most pathetic excuses in the Bible—perhaps in history: 'I said to them, let anyone who has gold, take it off, so they gave it to me; I threw it into the fire and there came out this calf.'

How sin deceives! Once you begin to turn away, you can deceive yourself. The sin of unbelief (verse 17) was of course *the* sin, that they did not believe that God purposed to deliver them into the promised land. How easily it happens; a splendid Christian fellow or girl in the church, but tempted. They shut their ears to the truth that they know so well. They begin to slip rapidly. They begin to live with somebody else, to go to bed with them. The truth is buried. 'Everybody's doing it. You're so old-fashioned, Mum! You're so old-fashioned, Dad! You don't know what it's like as a young person today.' And there it goes; down the slide.

There but for the grace of God.

I am sure that this is an agony to many of you, and I don't want to hurt you. But what I want to say is, wherever possible we must by the grace of God come alongside when we can see this beginning to happen. We may not be able to stop it, but we must not stand by and do nothing. And most of all we must pray.

3. Falling (4:1,11)

And then, it comes to falling. 'Since the promise of entering his rest still stands, let us be careful that none of you be found to have fallen short of it' (4:1); 'Let us, therefore, make every effort to enter that rest, so that no-one will fall by following their example of disobedience' (4:11).

What about the preservation of the saints? Don't we believe with all our heart, as Scripture says, that once we've turned to Christ 'we have passed from death to life'? Of course we do. Do we not know the scripture that 'none can pluck us from his hand'? Of course we do. Is it not true that God has given us eternal life, and that has begun now? Of course it's true. Isn't it true that 'nothing shall separate us from the love of God in Christ Jesus, neither life nor death nor principalities nor powers'? Yes, of course it's true. Thank God for it.

But you can't jump over this scripture. It's still here. If you and I are to be correct Christians, we are going to be based on Scripture in its entirety. And there are warnings here—warnings we may not feel fit in, because we believe in the preservation of the saints.

Calvin made quite a helpful distinction: 'Saints are

preserved not in spite of apostasy but from apostasy.' We may want to say of those who fall away like this that they were never saved. Yes, maybe that's the explanation. But whatever we feel about this doctrine, the important point is this: God has seen fit in His word to say to Christians (for this is addressed to Christians), 'Beware lest you fall away.' And if you're so hardened that you feel you could never fall away, you are probably more likely to do so. But if you're open in humility before the living God as a sinner saved by grace but still wrestling with the sinful nature within you, you will hold the wonderful doctrine of the preservation of the saints, but you'll never be complacent as you look at the sin that can so easily deceive—even in a Christian.

The 'rest' (4:4)

What is the 'rest'? 'On the seventh day God rested' (4:4). We're still in the seventh day. It's an entering into God's fellowship, and ultimately into heaven.

For me it was a wonderful release to realise that the Sabbath looked backwards towards creation in the rest, and the Lord's Day looks forward to heaven. If you only look backwards it becomes a very negative day; if you look forward it becomes a glorious day of anticipation of heaven. And you hold the two things together.

It's that glorious sense that God begins to give us already, 'the Spirit witnessing with our spirit that we are the children of God.' It's 'the firstfruits of the Spirit', to 'groan inwardly' as we wait for adoption as sons and the redemption of our bodies. It's that longing, that sense which the touch of God instils when He opens up heaven to us, takes us on to the transfiguration mount and lifts the veil, until our hearts are thrilled with it. Then we come back into the valley. But on we go! Because the 'rest' remains for the people of God.

The prevention of unfaithfulness (3:7–4:13)

How do we prod ourselves and one another so that we remain faithful? How concerned are we about the stage after conversion? I wonder how often, when we look back upon everything from eternity, we shall see that we failed to give ourselves to people at that point. How often do we regard converts as 'scalps', and then drop them?

That's just the moment when we need to give ourselves to them, for weeks and months to be alongside them, to care for them, to nurse them. This is the moment of after-birth. It is the most important moment. What has begun in them must begin to put down roots, so that God may begin to root them into His word and into His Spirit and into His power.

The prevention of unfaithfulness often comes right at the beginning. But notice, it is prevented in various ways.

1. By examination (3:12)
Not, fortunately, by an examination board, but by self-examination. 'See to it' (3:12). 'Take care', says the RSV; but 'See to it', NIV.

Do you ever stop and review your life, and actually ask yourself straight questions about where you are before God?

Some people I know take a day away—sometimes it's on their birthday—each year. Other people have a retreat each year, a special day or weekend apart. Away for the moment from fellowship and other people, just to be alone with God and to do a spiritual check-up, and say to God, 'Where am I? Have I slipped? Have I gone forward? What do You want to say to me?'—and actually to speak to Him direct about your life and where you are.

2. By encouragement (3:13)
What a lovely expression is used here: 'Encourage one another daily, as long as it is called Today.'

Have you encouraged someone this morning? You have to encourage one another—every day. What a lovely ministry it is—a word, a note, a letter, a thought, encouraging the good and true and positive things in another Christian's life.

When I went to work at All Souls, Langham Place, there was a man there, Harold Dodd, who had been a surgeon in Harley Street. He had just been ordained at the age of seventy; you can't do that now. He was a lovely man. He didn't develop many of the preaching skills necessary in the ministry, but what a man of encouragement! He was constantly sending little notes saying, 'Thank you for that, that was a lovely word...Thank you so much for that deed...Thank you for what you did there...' You could not but think of him as a man of encouragement.

What a lovely thing to be an encourager, not a critic— not a spiteful person always saying, 'Aha, aha!'

How grateful I am to Mr Yearsley, the army Scripture Reader. When I first went into the army, pretty tremulous in my Christian life, it was he who walked into the barrack room and said, eventually, 'Which of you are Christians?' You had to make a profession! He rescued me from my fearfulness. Without him I don't think I would be standing here today.

Thank God for the timely word of encouragement. Think of your young people going off to college for the first time. It's the most exposed moment in a young person's life. Free from home, they can do anything. Pray for them. Send a little note of love and encouragement (not a sermon!). Send them a box of chocolates or something; it's a way of remembering them.

I hope, my brothers and sisters, that you will be people who encourage one another daily. In the morning, say to God, 'Who can I encourage today?' Maybe pick up the phone and ring somebody; maybe at work—'Who can I encourage today?' Go into your office thinking, 'Who can I encourage today?' Don't be insufferable, but kind and thoughtful.

This is the advantage of fellowship; because notice that verse 13 speaks of sin as deceitful—and it's deceitful when you're on your own. You can imagine all sorts of things when you're on your own, but when you test it all in the fellowship, you can be strengthened.

3. By effort (4:11)

Sometimes we hear the phrase 'let go and let God'. There is some truth in that—but there's also no truth in that! Where is the fight of faith? Where is the wrestling against principalities and powers and the spiritual wickedness of this world? Where is the running of the race? Where is the endurance to the end? That has to be balanced with a trust in the living God. It is the effort of learning and thinking and training and developing and applying the faith towards a greater maturity and a greater usefulness for God. Never stop wanting to learn.

Thank God, many of you who are older than me are eager to know more! Thank God for you. I can remember being deeply moved by a clergyman in his very late eighties, when I was speaking at a convention in Australia. He came up afterwards with tears streaming down his face, held me by the hand and said, 'Thank you for what you've shown me of Jesus tonight.' I was in my forties, and I felt if I were nearly ninety and could actually be moved to tears by learning more about Jesus, what a mark it would be of a man who is going on!

This is the effort. Of course it's a blessed effort, to know more about the Lord. Do you train? Do you think? Can you apply the faith? We must, because (4:13) we have to look 'to whom we must give account'.

4. By exposure (4:12–13)

The phraseology runs memorably in these verses; it may have been from a poem current in the early church. The Scripture, that God has given us by His divine inspiration, is likened to a double-edged sword. Now, this is a short dagger. It's not something that will run you through and come out the other side. It's a surgeon's knife. It gets in to where the problem is. That's what the word of God does.

It is described here as living and active. People who don't believe look at it merely as a book. We see this as the place which the Holy Spirit brings alive and punches and refreshes us with in our own hearts. It's living!

Peter said that: 'You have been born again not of perishable seed but of imperishable, through the living and enduring word of God.' The word activates in us. It's made personally alive to us by the Holy Spirit's action. It isn't just a word, it is a living word, and that's why, when any person has taken it seriously in history, it has produced results in lives, in mission, in evangelism, in life.

The word goes on acting, doesn't it? Did you go on thinking about it yesterday? It doesn't stop when you walk out of the tent. You go on thinking about it. If God grabs you with something today, it will go on with you.

You remember Isaiah? 'My word... that goes forth from my mouth... shall not return to me empty. It shall accomplish that which I purpose and prosper in the thing for which I sent it' (Isa 55:10–11). God fulfils His purposes through His word, and nothing in the world or human life is untouched by it. Even creation came about by His word.

What does it do to us? Verse 12, again: 'It penetrates'.

Now, there's poetic language here—'dividing spirit and soul, joints and marrow'. It is surgical language. It's what is necessary to root out disease. It gets to the deep recesses of the heart, to our inmost thoughts, to our subconscious motives and to our hidden agendas. That's what the word does. Nothing else can do that. Nothing. Only the word of God can penetrate like that.

'It judges the thoughts and attitudes of the heart' (4:12). The word used here is a word used in wrestling: to take you by the throat, to overthrow you in wrestling terms. It's a wonderful thought. Martin Luther used to say that in order to come to us as our friend, God first comes to us as our adversary. The word grabs us.

Have you ever had that happen to you? Many times, perhaps. Maybe you've been in church, thinking all the world is fine, and suddenly God grabs you. The word comes to you; nobody else knows. It's between you and God. That's what the word does, isn't it? This is why, whatever anybody says, we know the word of God is active and living, and that it alone penetrates to the thoughts and intents of the heart. Let others go and pursue their weird theologies and bypasses! Nothing, nothing will penetrate the heart of man but the word of God.

The practice of faithfulness (4:14–6:20)

As I said earlier, the passage we've just been looking at, from 3:7, is really a digression. So 4:14 begins with a 'therefore'.

1. Be confident (4:14–16; 5:1–6)
There is a type of over-confidence that can be reprehensible—a cockiness about Christianity that sticks in other people's nostrils. But the confidence here is one of a quiet but firm settling into Christ and not into ourselves.

Look at the confidence in *the faith we profess* (verse 14). We're to hold it firmly, to master it and be strong in it, based on Jesus who has gone through the heavens.

It's this sense that the Lord on whom our faith is set is the Son of God, triumphant in resurrection and ascension, the King of kings and Lord of lords for ever. Our faith is not set in a piece of human philosophy, some meandering of man, but in Christ. And He is already in heaven, King of kings. Know it!

So often when I have to wrestle with extreme liberalism—that liberalism that derides the faith—I want to take its exponents into my diocese, into this country, into the world and say, 'Look, it works! The real faith works! This is the evidence of it!'

So have confidence in the faith. It is that alone which works, and transforms lives. Liberalism may affect the mind, but it doesn't transform life. And have confidence that He is the great—the superior—High Priest in heaven. Therefore, as Paul says, who can condemn? He is there, who saved us!

Then look at the confidence *to draw near* (4:15 to 5:6)—to approach the throne of grace direct.

That was a revolution, after all the business of the tabernacle and the temple and the curtain and the high priest, and all the paraphernalia of the sacrifice and so on! We must grasp the contemporary context of this. The Jews to whom this was written had to realise that a revolution had taken place; the curtain had been rent in two, the way into the holiest had been opened by the blood of Jesus. . . And he wants to say to them, 'Then be confident about it—use it. Don't stand there saying, "Isn't it marvellous!" Use the privilege you now have to approach the throne of grace direct, so that you may receive mercy and find grace in time of need.'

That boldness and openness is something in which we need constantly to renew ourselves. It's based, again (verse 13), on our openness to Him. Nothing is hidden from His sight. When we come to Him, we expose ourselves as well. Nothing should be held back as if God can't see the recesses of our life. Therefore, when we come, let us come openly, as we are.

We come, also, because He shared in our humanity and has sympathy. The Greek word is only used here in the New Testament, and means 'to suffer with'. He has understood our temptation; therefore we know He understands.

In 5:2 He is a High Priest with gentleness—the ability to see the problem and not to be repelled, to distinguish sin and the sinner, to respond so as not to condone sin but also so as not to bring angry over-judgement. This is our God.

So, firstly, we want to say to one another, be confident.

2. Be obedient (5:7–10)

Our Lord knew the need to pray. Verse 7: 'loud cries and tears to the one who could save him from death'. The rabbis distinguished three kinds of prayer: silent prayer, the voice raised involuntarily, and tears. Here it speaks of loud cries and tears. Of course, we think of Gethsemane, of the sweat falling as drops of blood: 'Lord, may this cup pass from me, but nevertheless, your will, not mine, be done.' What does it say in verse 7? 'He was heard'. But was He delivered? Oh no.

Now, this is a very important passage of Scripture, because it is saying that our God, our Saviour, our Lord, with loud cries and tears, in the battle of Gethsemane, was heard, but because He was obedient He submitted to the greater will of the Father. That is why He was not delivered from the cross; because the greater will of the Father was above what He longed for, or what His cry expressed at that time.

We have to learn that. Yes, you pray for healing and deliverance from suffering, but the greater 'yes' is to be obedient to God's purposes. And God so often glorifies Himself in the way in which Christians submit to suffering.

When you think of the greatest Christians you've ever

known, most of you will think of people who in the midst of suffering have glorified Jesus. How much we'd have lost of the wonderful witness to God that Joni's life bears, if she'd been healed instantly! Not that we wish her suffering on her; but what God has done through Joni is fantastic. This is the obedience, and what an example she has given us of it. It is that completeness (verse 9), that 'made perfect', that experience that in the midst of the great depths of suffering we're thrown on to God.

Sometimes God has to let the bottom drop out of our lives before we really learn to trust Him. That's what it means by being made perfect by suffering.

3. Be maturing (5:11—6:8)

a) The lack of maturity (5:11–14)

It's very easy in the Christian life to want comfort, to want the good feeling, the warm glow. But Christianity, my brothers and sisters, is comfortable and uncomfortable at the same time. God brings us His great comfort, but He challenges us in the midst of this evil world.

The baby (verse 14) does not easily see danger. It cannot discern between good and evil. Neither can baby Christians. And we need, steadily, fully, longingly to get forward off milk, on to the word, the truth of the word, the depth of the word.

They, it says in verse 11, were 'slow to learn'. They were not (and the Greek expression is vivid) leaning forward, hanging on to the word of God. They were laid back about it—'It doesn't matter very much!' If we're going to mature, it must be with the word.

b) The basics on which maturity can build (6:1–3)

He picks up the Jewish basics, which are relevant to Christians: repentance, faith, washings, resurrection.

But he goes on to say, 'You must get those foundations

laid.' That's what the basics of the faith are. We must get the foundations well and truly laid, or we won't be able to stand in the storm. But don't stop there! You must go on to maturity, he says.

c) The necessity of maturity (6:4–8)

Verse 8 recalls the words of our Lord in John 15:6, for these are solemn verses: 'If a man does not abide in me, he is cast forth as a branch and withers; and the branches are gathered, thrown into the fire and burned' (RSV).

This is the only place in the New Testament where we find the word that in verse 6 is translated 'fall away'. It means treachery, faithlessness, as in adultery. That's how it's described. 'I loved you, drew you to Myself and you were unfaithful.'

It's a fearsome passage. It speaks of crucifying the Son of God all over again and subjecting Him to public disgrace. Our hearts may well sink, particularly when we are told it is impossible to be brought back to repentance. Yet if this passage brings a son or daughter or relative to your mind—never give up! What is impossible with men is still possible with God. And your heart will pray and long and weep and cry for the one who you feel is trampling underfoot the blood of the covenant.

4. Be diligent (6:9–20)

a) Be expectant (verse 9)

What of? Of God's intentions.

He calls them 'beloved', because after such hard words he wants to grasp them, saying, 'I love you. Come on, I really think you're great! I know I'm being hard on you, but I do think you're wonderful.'

He speaks the truth with love. But he says, 'Be expectant! Lift up your heart! Realise that you're part of God and of God's loving intentions for you.'

Calvin said that nothing alienates the teacher from the student more quickly than the teacher making the student feel hopeless. How we need to try and see expectantly God's intentions for our lives!

b) Be 'e-valued' (verse 10)

—in His love.

I often used to criticise groups meeting together to discover what it meant to have self-love as Christians. But I realised how many people do not understand the value they have as the children of God. They have a low sense of personal worth. My brother and sister, that may be valid in the world's terms, but you're a Christian! You are infinitely valuable to the living God for ever. It's important, therefore, to stand back and be 'e-valued' by God, and see that you are of infinite preciousness to Him.

God is not unjust. He knows what you are doing, says verse 10. You're beavering away doing things for God quietly, and no one knows about it—but God does. Realise His valuation of you, which is very different from the world's assessments.

c) Be earnest (verses 11–12)

'Diligent' in the NIV—in commitment, going right on to the end of the road.

Some of you are old enough to remember Canon Guy King who used to come to Keswick. Remember what his favourite chorus was?

Go on, go on, go on, go on, go on, go on, go on,
Go on, go on, go on, go on, go on, go on, go on.

'Imitate', says the writer, 'those who have served before.'

d) Be enduring (verses 13–15)

Endure in the faith.

Abraham had a long wait to see God's promises

fulfilled—twenty-five years for a son. So he's set here as an example to us of patience and endurance in the faith.

e) Be encouraged (verses 16–20)

There are two ways in which you are to be encouraged. First, 'Take hold of the hope that you have.' Seize it; say, 'Nobody's going to take this from me. This is my eternal hope in Jesus Christ.' That is what you are to seize, as the RSV puts it, with a deliberate action of mind and heart, so that you're encouraged. Leap in the air occasionally, and say 'It's wonderful to be a Christian!' It's the glorious hope that is set before us. Seize it!

But there's something else: 'Let the hope seize you' (19–20). It's two-way traffic. The hope is spoken of as the anchor to our soul. Clement of Alexandria suggested there should be three Christian symbols: a dove, a fish and an anchor. How many Christians do you see wearing an anchor? Let's start a fashion!

We've looked at faithfulness, the pattern of it, the practice of it, and in between we've looked at unfaithfulness. Let's, then, face God afresh this morning.

We looked at Jesus yesterday; we've had to look at ourselves today. But that's part of Christianity. 'It is required of stewards that they be found faithful.' May God help you and me, so that at the end of our life, by the grace of God, He might say, 'Well done, good and faithful servant.' And in humility and streaming tears we might say, 'I have run the race, I have kept the faith, and henceforth there is laid up the crown of glory.'

'Therefore, holy brothers...fix your eyes on Jesus....*He* was faithful'—and so received the name of all Majesty.

3. Jesus and the New Covenant (Hebrews 7:1–10:18)

When I was six I was taken by early-morning train to visit my grandmother. We left in the dark and as we travelled through the countryside dawn broke. It was the first time I had ever seen it; I sat riveted at the window, watching the shadows gradually recede, the shapes of the farmhouses and the trees beginning to emerge, and everything gradually moving into glorious colour and then the full light of day.

God's revelation to mankind is like that. It moves from darkness into the full glorious light of Christ. On the way we see many shapes that eventually find their fulfilment in the full light of Christ.

That's what we're concerned about this morning: forms of sacrifice, of priesthood, of covenant, of being the people of God; all of which become flooded by the light of Christ. We will see how we move from the shadow-lands of the Old Testament to the reality-land of the New in Jesus Christ.

This was particularly important for the Jewish recipients. They lingered in the shadows. Obviously they wished to keep the Jewish forms and ceremonies. But they had to make the break, to move on to Christ, and to understand that it was all fulfilled in Him, that you didn't cease to be a Jew; you became a fulfilled Jew in Jesus Christ.

Sometimes in this study today we may begin to see the relevance to the situation of many even in our churches, who still live in shadow-land instead of reality-land. It is so easy to be carried away, even by fellowship, and somehow never come to Christ. It is very easy to stay with the symbols, the beauty, the stained glass (all of which I want to say are important: over-reacting by reverting to bare walls is not answering to God's creation); but when these cease to be an aid to worship, and become that upon which you are focused, then it's all gone wrong.

We are going to consider this in three ways: The superior Priest; the superior covenant; the superior atonement.

The superior Priest (chapter 7)

There are three ways in which the priesthood of Jesus Christ is superior to all the priesthood that went before.

1. The priesthood of Jesus Christ is primary

At the end of chapter 6, verse 20, it says: 'He has become a high priest for ever, in the order of Melchizedek.'

Gentile Christians may have felt the argument of chapter 7 to be somewhat irrelevant. For them and for us, the Lord Jesus Christ is clearly primary—Lord of all. Perhaps for us there is not the same need to argue as the writer argues; but his hearers did need to hear that argument, and so let's listen to it with them.

Melchizedek is not an everyday name for us. But let's listen with the ears of a Genesis 1 person, where the Bible begins. If we do not understand terms like 'Lamb of God', 'High Priest', 'suffering Servant', then much of the New Testament is lost on us. 'Behold the Lamb of God who takes away the sin of the world,' says John. What on earth does that mean, unless you understand the background to the statement?

The writer's argument is immensely important for the Jewish reader, who feels unable to discard thousands of years of history. He has to be shown how it all points to Jesus Christ. And we have to do that today, when we witness to those of our friends who are Jews.

The thrust of the argument is that Christ stands outside the Levitical priesthood, but is in the superior line of Melchizedek. Psalm 110, which is quoted here several times, was and still is a great Messianic psalm. The Lord of David is King over all, the Messiah who is to come, fulfilling kingship. In Psalm 110:4 this King is addressed thus: 'You are a priest for ever, in the order of Melchizedek.' So we need to know what it means, because it's quoted here in the New Testament.

It is a straightforward argument. Melchizedek is a separate line entirely from the Levitical priesthood, and the very name means 'king of peace, king of righteousness'. The writer gives five reasons why Melchizedek is superior.

1. He is without genealogy (verse 3)

Obviously he was born and he died, but the point is this: the way in which Melchizedek is introduced into holy writ, in Genesis 14, doesn't tell you anything about where he came from or where he went to. The writer says, in effect, 'This is so that you stand back from it and realise there is a timelessness about Melchizedek.' And Christ entering into that order enters into the timelessness of the priesthood.

2. His descent is not from Levi (verses 5–6)

Another reason lies in the word translated here as 'descent'—it's actually a word not used before. In Israel, if you were born as a male into the Levite tribe, you were automatically a priest. You didn't have to go to a theological college, you were automatically in the priestly line; and if you weren't in the Levite tribe you couldn't be a priest. They were the priests—full stop.

So the writer wants to say, Christ obviously isn't a Levite and He didn't descend from Levi (verse 6) but (verse 16) from Melchizedek. And notice what it says: not on the basis of a regulation as to His ancestry, but on the basis of the power of an indestructible life.

So the descent argument claims that He's in a line separate from the Levites.

3. He received tithes by personal authority (verses 4–5)

The tithing argument is this: Abraham (Genesis 14:17–20) gave tithes to Melchizedek. Abraham? Surely he was superior to Melchizedek? No, he gave tithes to Melchizedek.

And verse 5 says that the Levites collected tithes by right. 'We're Levites, you're under the law, you give us a tenth.' Melchizedek collected by personal authority. From law into that personal authority, reflecting that movement for us in Jesus Christ—even, of course, over giving.

People say, 'I'm not going to tithe, I'm not under law, so I'll give a pittance.' Oh no, it's the other way round. If you understand it, you're going to give more than a tithe. But you won't give because the law says it—that's only the standard from which we spring. You give because you are now under the personal authority of Jesus Christ and you love Him.

4. He blessed Abraham (verses 6–7)

The blessing argument (verse 6): 'Melchizedek blessed Abraham.' But Abraham is the father of the faith! Yes, but Melchizedek blessed him. Ah—then he must be more important; for verse 7 says the blesser is clearly superior.

As an aside, it's interesting that in Genesis 14, before

Melchizedek blesses Abraham he brings out bread and wine. The writer of Hebrews missed that one! He could have added another argument.

5. He was made a priest by God's oath, not by law (verse 20)

The oath argument: The Levites became priests without an oath, simply by law. 'I'm a Levite; I'm a priest.' But Melchizedek, and hence Jesus (verse 21), was a priest by God's oath. Psalm 110 again: 'The Lord has sworn and will not change his mind: you are a priest for ever.'

The point is this: God might change the law, but He will not go back on His oath. So though He may remove the Levitical priesthood, He will not remove the Christ priesthood, because He is in the line established by the oath of the living God.

2. The priesthood of Jesus Christ is permanent

Superiority lies not just in the primacy of His priesthood, but in its permanence. Let's look through the passage.

7:3: Melchizedek's record, without start or end, is compared to the true model, the Son of God, a Priest *for ever*. He is the Alpha and Omega.

7:17: 'You are a priest *for ever*.'

7:23–24: Other priests die and cannot continue in office. Jesus lives for ever, and therefore He has a *permanent priesthood*.

7:25: He continues to be always able to receive us, to save us, to intercede for us, to the end of time and into eternity. When you scrawl on the wall 'God is dead', we come back and say, 'He is alive for ever!' Our Priest is *permanent*.

The word 'permanent', in verse 24, is a legal word. It means 'non-transferable'. It's like writing across a cheque 'A/c payee—not negotiable'. And written across the cheque of the priesthood of Christ is the cross. This is not transferable. It is like the concept in science, of the foundational and unchangeable principles of the universe.

Verse 25: 'Therefore he always lives to intercede for them.' Remember Romans 8:34? 'He is at the right hand of God and is also interceding for us.' Not pleading our case for salvation before a reluctant God—Romans 8 blows that concept apart—but, as the Son to the Father, as enthroned King with the Father, in His love and concern for you and for me, my brothers and sisters. This is the prayer of the Lord of John 17; concern for His disciples. This is the prayer of the Lord for Peter before denial; not that he will not deny Him, but that his faith will not fail.

Don't you think it's a wonderful thing that Jesus is concerned for you and your progress, and intercedes for you? That's what it's about. So rejoice. He is High Priest for ever, and is always concerned for us. He intercedes for us for ever. He is permanent.

3. The priesthood of Jesus Christ is perfect

Of course perfection couldn't come by the Levitical priesthood. But Melchizedek is the king of righteousness.

How is this perfection seen (7:26–27)? It is in His being holy (and that means especially in relationship to God), blameless (free of all evil), pure (undefiled—the Lamb without spot, thus perfect to approach God), set apart from sinners (verse 27 says 'He does not need to offer sacrifices for his own sins'—because He has none, so He offers perfect manhood), and then He is exalted above the heavens, and that is the perfect Godhood now seeing the travail of His soul.

So this great comparison, of the perfection of our Priest with the imperfections of the priests with whom they had to deal, is ramming the point home to the Jews. These arguments will not make the same impact upon us, because unless our own background is Jewish, the issues are not of such direct concern to us. They will become much more so as we go on, but it's important to have these things in our mind now.

Verse 28 summarises: mere human high priests are weak, but the Son of God has been made perfect for ever.

Now, let's pause a moment. Of course there can be no more priests, in the Old Testament sense, since Jesus. The end of the whole sacrificial priesthood was in Jesus. He is the final High Priest, and any use of that term today can only be in the general sense: as a sort of shorthand for a presbyter, for someone leading services, for the sharing in the whole work and ministry of the priesthood of all believers into which we now enter. But if it's ever used in terms of a sacrificing priest standing between people and God, then it is not a New Testament usage.

This means that the Old Testament picture of priesthood ended once and for all with Jesus Christ. It was fulfilled in Him, and that is why the Jews who were listening to this letter had to be told to let the picture go: 'Let it go and turn to Jesus now as your High Priest, who is so much better. He is primary, He is permanent, He is perfect. What do you want to hang on to the old for?'

That's the force of it. What a boost, not just to the hearers here but to all Christians, as we bow in adoration to Jesus in this way!

The superior covenant (chapter 8)

The writer begins by saying (8:1), 'The point...is...' In other words, 'If you haven't followed the argument in chapter 7, at least let me tell you what it is.' We have every sympathy for his hearers, because chapter 7 isn't an easy one. Coverdale said, 'This is the pith', and it's a good way of putting it.

Chapter 7 leads us to this central argument about the

covenant. Most of us will know that 'covenant' means an agreement between people, and especially for us one between God and man—a contract signed and sealed. God has sealed the contract between Himself and man in blood, the blood of Jesus.

Think of how many ways the word 'covenant' occurs. For Noah the rainbow was the sign of the covenant. What next? Abraham, who was to be made the father of all people; again, sacrifice sealed that. For Moses, the covenant from Sinai—'You shall be my people'—was sealed, again, with sacrifice. And the covenant sign, circumcision, signified membership of the covenant people.

The same concept runs into the New Testament. And the word that accompanies 'covenant' is the word for 'covenant love'—*chesed*. It's one of the great words of the Old Testament. In the AV it was always translated 'mercy'—'His mercy endures for ever.' It's 'covenant love' (sometimes translated 'steadfast love'). It is the anchor word: the covenant does not just exist, it exists sealed in covenant love.

This is why in Hosea, for example, God says, 'I despise your sacrifices; I want your steadfast love, your *chesed*.' It is why in the Exile, when they were thrown out of Jerusalem, they said, 'How could it possibly have happened that the people of God have been thrown out of Jerusalem, and are here in exile in Babylon hanging our harps on the willow trees? How can we sing the Lord's song here?' The prophets wrestle with it, and in the end they come back to the one anchor rock, upon which their feet can stand and from which they can rebuild. And the anchor rock is: 'The covenant love of God cannot be broken.'

If you're miserable and want to feel more miserable, read Lamentations! But in Lamentations 3:23, in the midst of the misery—what happens? Suddenly: 'New every morning is your love; great is your faithfulness.' It comes like a tremendous pyrotechnic display on a dark night.

We rejoice in it in the New Testament: nothing, neither 'principalities, nor things present, nor things to come, nor powers . . . will be able to separate us from the love of God' (Romans 8:38–39, RSV)—that is covenant love.

This is the joy of the symbolism of covenant for us as Christians. And, of course, for us the sign is baptism, so that male and female can together share in the same covenant.

This new covenant is superior in different ways.

1. It is eternal

The context, fabric and impact of the new covenant is new, for it is in the eternal perspective. Most of the blessings of the Old Testament, as you know, were material—'If you follow God, you'll have your quiver full of children . . .', 'He will bless your going out and your coming in', for example. The New Testament moves us into a much deeper perspective. If you stay in the Old Testament, you get angry with God if He doesn't deliver what you want. It is the anger of a spoilt child. There's no place for that anger in the New Testament, because we've come into a new relationship as children to the Father, and we trust Him. If we stamp our feet, we're just petulant kids who need to grow up.

1. In its dimension (8:1–2)

Now, let's look at this eternity in its dimension. The priests of the Old Testament were in shadow-lands. The system of sacrifices offered by the priests according to the law was 'a copy and shadow of what is in heaven' (8:5). But this new covenant (verses 1–2) is set in eternal reality in heaven, at the right hand of the throne of Majesty:

God's eternal sanctuary, set up and made by God, the Lord.

The difference is between the dimension of mere earthly thinking and the dimension of heaven, of eternity.

2. In its Mediator

But we must look not only at its dimension, but also its Mediator: who He is and what He did.

Who He is (verse 6): His ministry is superior because it's no longer that of a mere mortal. That is why our first study's emphasis on who Jesus is was so important. Beware of those who want to confine Jesus to mere humanity! Only as Lord of all can He take us into the eternal reality of covenant love for ever, and not just keep us in the shadow of hope.

What He did (verse 1): He sat down, His work was complete.

Verse 3. It was not an ongoing offering, for He offered Himself. Look back to 7:27—'He offered himself once and for all.' So here is the force of it: He is the Mediator of the covenant because of who He is and because of what He did. He is the Son of God, and He offered Himself as the sacrifice once and for all.

3. In its promises (verse 6)

It is founded on better promises. The old was a covenant by law with promises, the new is a covenant of promise— of being eternally a member of God's people, not just on earth. When you stay in shadow-land you can only think of it in earthly terms. But the promises of the covenant are eternal, breaking through the bonds of death. So we rejoice to sing, 'Standing on the promises of Christ, my Saviour'.

2. *It is internal*

In verse 8 we pick up the wonderful promise of Jeremiah 31—the moment in the Old Testament when the New Covenant was foretold. It was to be totally different: hence Jesus describes the broken bread and the wine poured out as the 'new' covenant. And the author of Hebrews rightly connects Jeremiah 31 to the cross.

Now here, then, we have an internal aspect. Look at 8:10 and let it remind you of that covenant in Jeremiah 31: 'I will put my laws in their minds, and write them in their hearts.' That covers the intellect, the will, the affections. Romans 8:3: 'What the law was powerless to do...God did by sending his own Son.'

This is the Holy Spirit dimension. Jesus says in John 14, the Spirit was with you, then—He will be in you. This is the Pentecostal transformation. Every Christian is a Pentecostal Christian! If you haven't got the Spirit, you're not a Christian.

Romans 8 speaks of the internal covenant by the Spirit. The Spirit frees us from sin's bondage, the Spirit brings our spirit to life and peace. The Spirit assures us. The Spirit helps us cry 'Abba, Father.' The Spirit gives us the foretaste of glory. The Spirit intercedes in us. The Spirit gifts us, leads us, and supremely opens God and Christ to us.

Isn't it wonderful? No wonder people who just stick in an intellectual faith and don't know what it is to be born again of the Spirit of God can't understand what on earth we're talking about! You say, 'It's wonderful to be a Christian'—they say, 'What's wonderful about it?' The problem of Nicodemus is still with us today, inside and outside the church.

I remember in my early twenties the thrill of sitting up into the night and finding Bible passages with which I had struggled leaping out at me. And today the Bible is still fresh, vital and invigorating. Myrtle and I read the same passage each morning, separately. We often say to each other over breakfast, 'Isn't that passage terrific?'

Only the Spirit can do that. The covenant is internal.

3. It is personal

There are two things you cannot do on your own—marry, and be a Christian. You're always incorporated into the whole body of Christ, the family of God. But it is also a very personal relationship that we have with our God.

This is the intention: in the new covenant we're going to know Him, not just in the more distant way of the old covenant (verse 9). How? Verse 12 tells us. By the removal of the barrier between man and God. Only when sin is dealt with by the blood of Jesus are we open to God, and only then does the Spirit flood in.

Conversion and the rebirth of the Spirit are identical—they must be. That's when the cloud is removed and the sunshine pours in upon us. This is the offer to every human being.

4. It is universal (verse 11)

Although people could be attached to Judaism, and the intention of Abraham was that all the families of the earth should be blessed, it was nonetheless a nationalistic faith, and remained so. The old covenant was limited by this, but the new would fulfil Abraham's call for all the nations to be blessed. And when Paul argues about the wonder of salvation in Romans 4, he goes back to the Abrahamic promise and covenant in explanation of the gospel.

So the 'all' of verse 11 has far wider application than Israel. There is no limitation of the covenant to the Jews. The readers had to see that now God's covenant was universal, for Jews and Gentiles alike.

And today, with the increased influence and power of multi-faith events, of militant Islamic nationalism and the rest, we need constantly to say to one another that Jesus alone is the Messiah, that He alone is the way of salvation, that only through Him can you be saved. His is the name above every name, and only in Jesus Christ the Son of God and the new covenant wrought in His blood, can men and women be saved.

This new covenant is superior to the old because it is eternal in its dimension, Mediator and promises. It is internal, personal and universal.

So (verse 13) the old covenant was obsolete and ageing and would soon disappear. Rejoice in the wonder of the new covenant, that Jesus has wrought for us!

The superior atonement (9:1–10:18)

This is the climax of the arguments. We now move fully from shadow-lands to reality-land, in the atonement.

The excitement of the author is like that of a preacher getting so carried away that words, concepts and joyful convictions tumble out. It doesn't make an expositor's task easy! So what I have decided to do is to handle it in two ways, as you'll see.

1. The shadow of the old

Chapter 9:1–10 speaks particularly on the shadow, but it is more than that.

Look at verse 8 of chapter 9. 'The Holy Spirit was showing by this.' God is a wonderful communicator. He loves to use visual aids. The stupidity of those who deny the virgin birth and the empty tomb is the stupidity of not realising that God has done it in this way to make it so abundantly clear for even a child to understand, and they have messed us up with their stupid confusing statements about it.

And here we have the wonderful pictures that come in the Old Testament, the ceremonies, the sacrifices, the priesthood; not in themselves unprofitable, but nonetheless not the final thing. What does it mean to be God's people? It has to do with sin, forgiveness and holiness. Later we shall be reading that 'these people did not receive the things promised, they only saw them and welcomed them from afar'. Well, we have the privilege of being on this side of the cross.

Now, we're reminded of some of the symbolisms.

Verse 2: the tabernacle (notice, not the temple; I think he has his Gentile readers in mind here because he explains things here that Jews would have known). Verse 2: the first room, the holy place. Verse 3: the second curtain. Verse 4: behind that, the most holy place where the ark was, of the covenant and the commandments— the place of atonement. Now in that (verse 6) was the outer room into which the priests went regularly, and (verse 7) the inner room where only the high priest went once a year with blood. I wonder whether you knew that the sacrifice was offered in the outer room? And when he went into the inner room, the holy of holies, he went with the blood on him as the mark that the sacrifice had been given outside the veil.

The blood (verse 13) was of goats and bulls sprinkled on the unclean, to make them outwardly clean. Verses 19–22: the sprinkling of the blood at the Sinai covenant and the giving of the commandments was the way in which God did it.

And in verse 20, the sign of the covenant: blood was associated with the making of the covenant. Obedience was involved: 'which God has commanded you to keep' (verse 20). It was this covenant love which they broke and about which God so strongly took them to task in Hosea.

These Old Testament sacrifices were repeated 'endlessly' (10:1). It went on and on, year after year, because it couldn't make the people lastingly right with God.

Think of the equivalents today—people going off to be washed in the Ganges, to go on their knees to Mecca— and Christians, or, at least, people in the church, who have no assurance of salvation, even those who go forward at rallies for the umpteenth time just to make sure— that's all Old Testament. And the Old Testament covenant (10:11) could never take away sins.

Today various theologians denigrate the atonement. The cross is to them only an example of love and helplessness—what man does to man, not a sacrifice for sins. They object strongly to those of us who speak of it so, yet strangely they go to communion and take the broken body and blood of Christ in symbolism in the bread and wine. They believe that all will be saved regardless, and they are derogatory to all who believe in the atonement. They don't like the idea that man is a sinner. In fact, they don't even like the idea of original sin.

Well, the best thing for us to do is to get on with knowing the truth and spreading it. So it's particularly important to realise that the atonement was initiated by God from the beginning. That's the force of Hebrews. It wasn't a new idea. God went to enormous lengths to prepare the way by the mighty visual aids of Old Testament ritual and sacrifice, and none of it—*none* of it— would have been necessary if you could simply be made right with God without the sacrifice and the repentance.

Thus the spelling out of Old Testament symbolism adds enormous strength to the teaching of the atonement and is evidence of its enormous importance to God in His saving of humanity. So, though in Christ we see the reality, the shadow-land is important to us to help us understand the significance of the reality. Let us now sketch it out quickly.

2. The reality of the new

1. Christ is there

He has entered the most holy place (9:11), He has entered heaven itself and He is in God's presence for us (9:24).

That's what it's all about, the holy of holies. Yes, He's there in heaven. Rejoice in it! We are told (9:15) that if we are in the new covenant, our own eternal inheritance is assured; it is guaranteed, because the Saviour is there. We are encouraged to press on, looking to Jesus (as we shall do in chapter 12), the author and perfector of our faith who is already there in heaven.

It means He is ready to help us to follow. The barrier of the curtain has gone. The sadness of those modern extreme liberal theologians who have now got to the point of even doubting life after death—God help them! They reject the New Testament as first-century irrelevance. God help them! It's the most powerful and life-transforming word in the whole of the world.

2. Christ's shed blood is effectual

It is His own blood (9:12), and therefore it obtained eternal redemption.

The sacrifice had been outside the walls of the city, in the world (we shall return to that tomorrow). And then He entered heaven because of that shed blood upon Him. The blood is the mark of death (9:16). It's evidence that the sacrifice has been made.

Chapter 10:4 says 'it is impossible for the blood of bulls and goats to take away sins', but in the blood of Jesus we are cleansed. That is the difference: the old could not take sins away.

As Isaac Watts put it,

Not all the blood of beasts
On Jewish altars slain

Could give the guilty conscience peace
Or wash away the stain.
But Christ, the heavenly Lamb,
Takes all our sins away;
A sacrifice of nobler name
And richer blood than they.

Precisely Hebrews! And (9:14) it isn't outward but inward; entering into Christ's death cleanses our consciences. It changes us within. Instead of self, we are to serve Him, cleansed by the precious blood of Christ. It's not enough to rejoice in being saved unless it is effectual in our life, and in our service of the living God.

And so we should ponder here the seriousness of sin, that required such a measure of sacrifice and death in the Old Testament and supremely in the cross of Christ. And how we must hurt Him, if we profess salvation and go on sinning as if we are not saved! His blood is intended to cleanse you within.

He urges us to witness today. Today man wants to avoid the idea of sin. He wants to argue that what's wrong with man is merely the influences of his genes or his environment. He goes to fatalism, to the occult, to astrology, and is more concerned about which planet he thinks he's born under than that there is a Saviour of the world who shed His blood for him. And you and I are called in the midst of all this to bring people to see that only through the shed blood of Jesus Christ can they be redeemed from such false egocentric thinking.

3. Christ's sacrifice was 'once for all'

It's the vital phrase that comes many times in Hebrews: in 9:12, 26, 28 and 10:10, 11. The shadow has gone! The reality has come! It is once for all! It is the great statement of the atonement, never to be repeated. The finality of this was spelt out on Good Friday, when He said, 'It is finished.' The resurrection evidenced it, but it was on the Good Friday it was finished. And in the shadow picture we're pointed to the physical position of the High Priest; in reality, Christ sits down because His work is finished (10:12).

Thank God for the Church of England Prayer Book, for instance, which speaks of: 'Jesus Christ who came to suffer death upon the cross for our redemption, who made there by His one oblation of Himself once offered a full, perfect and sufficient sacrifice, oblation and satisfaction for the sins of the whole world.' You can't say it better than that, can you? Even in the Alternative Service Book, which some people don't like, in every eucharistic prayer it says 'once for all'.

So, participating in the Lord's Supper, the Holy Communion, the Eucharist, is to be a glorious assurance. We don't need to make new sacrifices. We remember and identify with His once-and-for-all sacrifice. It doesn't depend on us, but upon Jesus who died for us.

And without thus grasping the atonement, people lack assurance; and what a tragedy that is.

4. Christ died as a ransom (9:15)

'Ransom' is a word that comes in Mark 10:45: 'The Son of man came to give his life as a ransom for many.' It's an aspect of the atonement, a way of expressing man's liberation from bondage to sin that has power over him and can only be broken by Christ's death for him.

Ransom means a lot to us today. We think of those who are hostages in various parts of the world. When they are released by a ransom, they are set free. And so in the New Testament we are set free 'from the sins committed under the first covenant' (9:15). The power of sin is broken. Do you believe it? Do you live as if it is?

5. Christ obeyed (10:5–10)

In the Old Testament, priests obeyed the demands of the law; in the New Testament Christ obeys the Father.

From a child He wanted to do the will of His Father. At the well with the woman of Samaria, He said, 'My meat is to do the will of him who sent me.' In Gethsemane, it was the will of the Father that was paramount. Here in 10:7— 'I have come to do your will, O God.' The wonder of it! 'By this we have been made holy,' it says. We have all the benefits of this.

Similarly, He says to us, 'If you love Me, keep My commandments. If you're the Bride, be without spot. Grow in holiness of life, dedication, obedience to do His will.' And, however much we may reason through what is right and wrong, it is His will that matters most.

Recently we were talking with some relatives who had the possibility of going either to a post in Africa or one in France. We sought for a long time to help them think it through. At the end, the logical choice seemed to be France. In the middle of that night I woke up. It was like neon signs across the bed. 'Africa, Michael! Africa it is! Blow your logic—it's Africa!' That's where they now are. God's wisdom is above our logic. They were obedient and went.

6. Christ will emerge once more (9:28)

They held their breath in case the priest didn't return.

> Come in O My glorious Priest,
> Hear we not Your golden bells?

says the hymn. Well, he didn't actually have bells, but the picture's all right. They held their breath in case he would not come back again.

The New Testament says, 'You've no need to hold your

breath—He *is* coming again!' And we are already at the end of the ages since His first coming.

7. He waits for His enemies (10:13)

The nations are His heritage, He who is to be pre-eminent. That day is coming.

If there is delay in His coming, says Peter, it is to give time for more to be saved. But that day will come when He hands over the kingdom to God the Father, after He has destroyed all dominion, authority and power. 'For He must reign till He has put all enemies under His feet, and the last enemy to be destroyed is death.' Many people will rail against Christ, but no one can dethrone Him. He is Lord. He is King. He is our High Priest, the Creator of the New Covenant, the one who by His own blood has wrought our atonement by which we are saved, and for all eternity we shall praise Him as the one deserving of the name of all Majesty.

4. Fix Your Eyes on Jesus — Be God's Persevering People (Hebrews 10:19–13:25)

Well, we now take off on the last leg of our flight through Hebrews.

We are to persevere

If only we could have just slipped into heaven yesterday! We almost got there; we almost took off at the end, at the final view of the triumph. But I'm afraid we have to come down from the Mount of Transfiguration into the valley. And this is the great thing about Hebrews—it lifts us up, as we know God for who He is, and then how to be faithful, and then what He's done for us, and now what it means to persevere.

Christianity is not just the rejoicing in the salvation He brings, but the persevering to the end. And that's why it's so good that Romans gives us the theology of the gospel, then brings us straight to the practicalities. Ephesians does it, Colossians does it, Hebrews does it.

There are many 'therefores' in this epistle. In 2:1 (though not in the NIV, but it is there): Who is Jesus? If you know who He is, 'therefore you hear his word'. In 3:1: Jesus shared our humanity and temptations, 'therefore, turn to him for help'. In 4:1: The promise of eternal rest still stands, 'therefore, do not lose out'. In 4:14: We have a High Priest in heaven, 'therefore, hold to the faith'. In 6:1: We need solid food, not milk, 'therefore, aim at maturity'. In 7:25: Jesus has a permanent priesthood, 'therefore, he is able to save those who come to him'. In 10:5: The blood of animals cannot remove sin, therefore, Christ came to offer himself.

It's a favourite word of our writer, and here it crashes in to introduce this final section: if you really grasp the meaning of the superior priesthood of Christ, the covenant atonement in Him mean—*therefore* you will work it out. He reminds us of the reasons.

Verse 19: The blood of Jesus, the sacrifice for sins once for all. Verse 20: There is a new and living way—the word means 'absolutely new'; how much that now means to us in the context of such events as the destruction of the Berlin Wall. But for Christ, the temple curtain, the way into the holiest, was ripped in two by His body. Finally, verse 21: the high priestly status of Jesus, a great Priest over the house of God.

All this, he reminds us, compels the response that whatever the circumstances and problems of life in the world, we should be God's persevering people.

Now follows a check-list of thirteen items.

With cleansing (10:22, 26–31)

Faith (in verse 22) is the faith that fully accepts the glorious fact of the atonement and is assured. Assurance is inseparably linked to understanding that you are forgiven. If you do not grasp the fact that you are forgiven through the atonement of Christ, you can never have assurance.

This is why, so often, we find ourselves frustrated. You try and explain the gospel to someone, you go over it in the simplest possible terms, you repeat it and repeat it and at the end they say, 'Oh yes, I see, I've got to try harder.'

That's how I lost my hair—I tore it out so many times in that frustration!

Until you see that He has died for you, you cannot have assurance. It's not through trying harder, it's through coming, as I often remind people at Confirmation—you come to the Communion with an empty hand.

> Nothing in my hand I bring,
> Simply to Thy cross I cling.

You renew it every time you come.

Many people look for extra ways of assurance: going forward at evangelistic rallies, or seeking some extra experience without which one doesn't have the 'full thing'. People run after this and that: 'Have you heard what's going on? We'd better go and see.' God forgive us! We're like children rushing about after the latest thing. Often it's because we don't have rooted assurance that we are washed and cleansed. Baptism is meant to symbolise that full-scale bath once and for all (verse 22), the sprinkling and the washing.

And so the Christian who has grasped assurance should not go on being deeply disturbed by the memory of past sins. They are washed away, they are removed from us as far as the East is from the West. Believe it! Oh, sometimes I want to shake some Christians! Believe it! He has washed you.

But, although that's a glorious truth and one we rejoice in and need to grasp, we need also a constant cleansing. You remember the battle in John 13, the foot-washing: Jesus says, 'If I don't do this, you don't have any part with Me;' and Peter, typically, says, 'Then if I'm going to have it, I'll have the lot!' Jesus says, 'No, you've had the bath; but you need the foot-washing, the constant readiness to be cleansed day by day.'

Now, my brothers and sisters, this comes nearer home. The liturgy of the Church of England teaches us in its morning, evening and communion services that we must begin with confession—what we have done and should not have done; what we have not done and should have done. As somebody said in the days when everybody used the Prayer Book: 'I don't like going to church, because every time I go I have to describe myself as a miserable offender.' (Or, as the ASB puts it, 'We are truly sorry.')

We may well react to the idea of confession. But do you confess? How often in the last fortnight have you actually repented of sin? I'm afraid we don't often take sin seriously day by day. We believe in the foot-washing, but it's so easily neglected. How often do we bring our lives before God, laying the unknown faults before Him for cleansing, as well as those we know about?

The Christian who's going to persevere needs to take daily cleansing seriously. And if this isn't part of your devotional life yet and you take that thought home from Keswick, it will have been worth coming.

The seriousness and horror of sin in the Christian are spelt out in a severe warning (verses 26–31). His concern is to deliver a sharp shock to those in the church who are slipping back into non-Christian ways. It's not necessarily saying that his readers had fallen, but he sees them as in danger of doing so. So he therefore delivers a horrific shock: 'Do you realise what this could go to?'

The reference here is to Deuteronomy 17. The Old Testament distinguished between intentional and unintentional sin. Here (verse 26) it is intentional, if we deliberately keep on sinning. What was the sin? In the early church the concern was about post-baptismal sin, in particular sexual irregularity. Today it would refer perhaps to Christians who deliberately sin in this and other ways.

Verse 29 is uncomfortable reading. Doesn't it make

you shudder? Don't get carried away with the preser-
vation-of-the-saints idea, just realise this is to shock you
and me—to realise that Christians can slide towards this
rejection, almost, of all that the grace of God has done in
them.

Cleansing is an answer to that; a deep desire to be
cleansed day by day and to have your life open to God.

With hope (10:23,32–39)
The proper response to Jesus as the great High Priest is to
take hold of hope. The Authorised Version here strangely
puts 'faith', but the word is 'hope'. And we must hope
'unswervingly'. Nothing must deflect Christians from the
hope that God has given them. That's the force of it.
Extreme liberalism in theology; doubts; the media; the
events of life, and criticisms of the church shouldn't rock
you. The hope is certain.

But it needs perseverance (32–39). They have a good
track record. They have stood their ground (32–34).
They've even faced persecution. They've supported those
in prison. They've joyfully accepted confiscation of property. But now they've come to a rather comfortable period
in their Christian life with nothing to fight against. And
that's when the danger comes.

It's all very well when we're all united in battle, but
when peace comes it's sometimes more difficult to come
together. And the writer is saying, 'You are now in some
danger because you are not doing so, you don't have to at
the moment, therefore be careful, be careful.'

And he says (verse 37) that hope should strengthen
perseverance because it knows Christ is coming and you
and I will stand before Him. That is a tremendous force
for us, to serve Christ; however much I have to stand
against criticism and so on, the one thing I do know is that

Christ knows the truth. And whatever the national news-papers—or some Christians—may say, Christ knows the truth and in the end I'm answerable to Him.

But it also reminds me that I am answerable to Him, not for salvation but for the job He's given me to do, to do it to the end, unswervingly, because hope reminds me not only of the joy set before me but of the responsibility of the task He's given me, to serve Him in this one life He's entrusted to me.

With encouragement (10:24–25)

How much we need each other, to strengthen per-severance! Verse 24 says 'spur one another on', in the NIV. The Greek word is normally used of people who provoke others to exasperation by the kind of things they say, and I reckon there was somebody like that in the church—there usually is in any church. And he says to them, 'All right, you want to provoke people to exaspera-tion; why not steer it in another direction? If you *have* to keep speaking to people about everything, why don't you encourage them instead of criticising?'

Calvin commented on verses 24 and 25, 'There is so much peevishness in almost everyone that individuals, if they could, would gladly make their own churches for themselves.' We know only too well what Calvin meant. Some sympathise with C.S. Lewis: 'Though I liked clergy-men as I liked bears, I had as little wish to be in the church as in the zoo. It was a wearisome get-together affair, the bells, the crowns, the umbrellas, the notices, the bustle of perpetual arranging and organising. Hymns were and are extremely disagreeable to me, and of all the musical instruments I liked, I liked the organ the least.'

I'm sure he's been in my congregation! Perhaps such people are in the mind of the writer to the Hebrews. Verse 25: 'You mustn't give up meeting just because you don't happen to like something.' As I often used to say at All

Souls, 'If there's not something in this service that you don't like, we've probably got it wrong.'

You don't give up because you haven't got what you wanted out of the service, he says. 'You go there also to give to other people, you go there to be part of the fellowship; if you're not there, you're breaking the fellowship. You could be a real help to somebody else. But instead you're staying at home and saying, "I don't like it any more." '

With faith (10:39—12:3)

God's persevering people do not shrink back, for they are God's believing people, saved by faith.

God's anchor to faith (11:1–3)

Now, see what it is saying. It is saying this: certainty is intended by God.

On all sides we have to put up with the liberal theologians and others who keep saying, 'There is no certainty about anything.' They claim that those who express certainty have closed their minds. They say it of me. Or, as one prominent bishop said in the Synod the other day, 'They have a psychological need.' So has he. It's the cheapest jibe in the world to say, 'You don't agree with me, therefore you've closed your mind.' In fact, modern liberalism is the most aggressive (in the sense of not allowing anybody else to think) of all the theologies around. So, let's come back and see: certainty is commended by God.

Of course, if you don't have a living faith, you're not going to have certainty. But faith is met by God, by His Spirit, His inward opening up of His truth to us. And this certainty is also here in these first few verses, founded by God Himself. It has a God-creator dimension to everything.

Creation was out of nothing (verse 3). It's important that this word is here. It counteracted the heresies of the day about creation being moulded from existing, marred matter. The truth of Scripture is that creation was out of nothing and it was by the word of God alone. That's the force of the Scriptures. It's that which is expressed, for me, in Haydn's Creation, when the words are sung 'Let there be light'. Every voice, every instrument—'light'!

God said it, and it happened. That's the force. And so this certainty springs from the fact that this is God's world. Faith is anchored, therefore, into this God-dimension of creation, and of the sure hope of God's eternal heaven ahead.

God's attitude to faith (11:6,16)

It pleases Him. Isn't that lovely? It pleases Him. Do you think of your God being pleased because you believe? Isn't that lovely, this faithfulness? 'If he shrinks back,' says 10:38, 'I will not be pleased with him.' But 11:6 says, 'Without faith it is impossible to please God.' Faith—that means believing God is God.

I sometimes have said across the years to congregations, 'Do you really believe in God? You're acting as if you can work out what you think God might be able to do. You're not acting as if you believe in a God who is able to do exceeding abundantly above all that you ask or think. You're limiting God!'

I went to one church where they were involved in a building project. One man said, 'I will never ever let this church go forward on a building project until we have all the money in the bank.' And I said to him, 'Then you'll never do it.' And they never have.

Faith reaches out when God has called, and God is pleased to honour the faith that trusts Him as God. It brings His approval (verse 16) in the persevering of the saints of Old Testament history: 'Therefore God is not ashamed to be called their God, for he has prepared a city for them.'

'Not ashamed'—how ashamed He must be at faithless Christians.

God's accolades for faith (11:4–38)

Let me give you the categories briefly.

1. Devotion faith (verses 4–6). Look at it in chapter 11. Abel, who brings the best. Cain, who just brought anything. That was the difference, wasn't it? Abel went out and chose the very best of his flock. Cain said, 'Oh, I suppose we've got to have an offering. I'd better put something in it.'

And then there's Enoch, the mystical holy man who (the Septuagint says) walked with God in a lovely close relationship. But let me tell you something about Enoch. He was a Sethite. It was a very inferior line, inferior even to the line of Cain. You can't get much lower than that! Yet God gives Enoch the top honours award.

Because you simply don't have to have brains, or artistic ability, or the ability to play a guitar with your big toe, to be honourable to God. Those are lovely gifts when they are entrusted to you, but I want to encourage those of you who feel, 'Well, my gifts are very quiet, really. I don't do all these things... But I do serve God day by day.' You're probably the salt of the earth in your street, and people say, 'Ah, isn't he, or she, marvellous?' No one's going to write it up, but God knows.

And I want to tell every 'Enoch' in this tent today, that God knows. And when He gives out the honours, it won't be to the bishops. Goodness me, we'll be at the back! It will be to the Enochs of this world, the Sethites of today, because of their devotion. They simply love the Lord with all their heart, and their life demonstrates it.

2. Daring faith (verses 7–19). Noah, against all the

odds, in face of mockery, he dared; the first man in the Bible to be called righteous. Abraham, going into the unknown, a pilgrim life, offering Isaac. He dared. How many people have gone in that tradition down through the centuries, who have dared for Jesus Christ?

Recently I attended the commissioning of the new *Logos II* ship. There has been some daring! Whoever would have thought of having a ship to go round the world!

A daring faith! It's very exciting to read about.

3. Determined faith (verses 20–31). All these overlap to some extent, of course. A marvellous accolade to Joseph. After all, one of the most brilliant prime ministers in history. And what does Hebrews say about him? 'He gave direction concerning his bones'! Do you think *The Times* obituary might have done something different from that? The one thing that stood out about him was not that he was the prime minister, but that he had a determined faith that God was going to bring His people into the land He'd promised.

Moses, my hero. 'He persevered because he saw him who is invisible' (verse 27). Passover—the Red Sea— how many incredible things he faced in his humanity, and how God had to push him! 'Stand still and see the salvation of the Lord,' he says, but read on: God says, 'Don't stand still; get on with it. Go on in faith, and then the waters will part.'

And Joshua—once a day round Jericho, and then seven times, in heat much greater than the unusual hot weather we're having now. You have to be determined to do that. Determined faith.

4. Deliverance faith (verses 32–35). Gideon, Samson, Daniel and so on. There are many paperbacks about Christians today who've been in similar circumstances. And they're very exciting to read!

5. Disaster faith (verses 35–38). But I'm afraid there are some more verses, describing what I have called 'disaster faith'. Not disaster from God's viewpoint, but from man's.

This is more uncomfortable! We love the conquest, the deliverance, the excitement; but this is different. Christians who want triumphalism, who cannot admit to any defeat, any problem, any doubt, any burden, any heartache, any difficulty, who have to live a charade of always being on top of things—Lord save you, you're going to crash. You have to be honest before God, and Hebrews 11 mercifully balances the picture.

It includes deliverance, of course, but now it mentions torture (verse 35). The word used means somebody being stretched on a rack.

Chained and imprisoned, stoned, sawn in two—tradition says that's what happened to Isaiah—killed by the sword—and then, hear it: 'They went about in sheepskins and goatskins, destitute, persecuted and ill-treated—the world was not worthy of them. They wandered in deserts and mountains, and in caves and in holes in the ground.'

By faith! By faith!

Yes, we can take the devotion, yes, we can take the deliverance, yes, we can take all the exploits. But this when there was no deliverance, when there was death, there was torture, there was persecution, they were smashed into the ground—by faith?

Yes, says the writer: and which is the greatest faith of all? The one when you're riding high—or the one when you're being persecuted because you're a Christian? In the end, I think we would admit that the most wonderful Christians we have known have been those who in the midst of suffering and pain shone for Jesus.

Many of these incidents refer particularly to the inter-testamental years, when the Maccabees violently sacked Jerusalem. Something like eighty thousand were killed.

But think about this: all this (verses 39–40) happened before Jesus! You and I have Jesus and the Holy Spirit and the knowledge of the gospel and of the church. This faith was before that.

God's application of faith (12:1–3)

So God applies it. He says, 'Look at it; and don't collapse' (12:3). 'Don't collapse before you get there.' You've got all eternity to recover.

1. *By looking to examples.* You keep on, and you are encouraged to keep on by the way in which you look to the examples of those who've gone before, the surround of the great cloud of witnesses. They are saying, 'We've been through it and it's worth everything.' Christian biographies are wonderful things to read; they meant a great deal to me in my early days. So we are even told (11:4) that Abel still speaks though dead; their lives speak to us.

2. *By letting go of what hinders us (verse 1)*—the attitudes, the sin, the materialism.

3. *By looking to Jesus (verse 2).* He is supremely the inspirer, as we see how He ran, suffered, endured and triumphed. That's why it's so good to follow the Church calendar as through the year, every year, we remember all the events of Christ's life.

4. *By looking to heaven (verse 2).* The finishing tape ahead, the foretaste of heaven, the joy of it; like the swimmer, lifting the head occasionally to make sure the finishing line's still there.

All this is exciting—a familiar passage—and I'm going to move straight on from it. It's in the Bible to encourage us all with faith.

With training (12:4–13)

The means of training is God's discipline. It starts by reminding the people of Scripture (verse 5)—always a good place to start. The writer refers to Proverbs because, of course, Christ could not be used as an example of being disciplined by suffering.

'Punishes' (verse 6) is not actually in the original Hebrew version of Proverbs 3. The translation here is an unfortunate echo of the Greek translation of the Old Testament rather than the Hebrew. It is better to read it as 'disciplines'.

Discipline is the mark of sonship. Jerome said, 'The greatest anger of all is when God is no longer angry with us when we sin, when we have become unteachable.' For God has to discipline us. Often the result is self-pity and anger: 'Why has this happened to me?' But, look at it.

Verse 5 says, don't make light of it, don't lose heart over it. Verse 7 says, endure it. Verse 10 says, it will be for our good and our holiness. Verse 11 says, it will be for our righteousness and peace.

So what we need to do is to strengthen one another (verse 12), when we are going through problems and difficulties. Especially, we need to strengthen the weak-kneed Christians, not condemning them but helping them become healed of their wrong attitudes (verse 13). Isn't that lovely?

With holiness (12:14–17)
Holiness is necessary to see the Lord, says verse 14. 'Blessed are the pure in heart for they shall see God.'

Bishop Westcott said, 'Holiness is the preparation for the presence of God.' Unholy living blocks us off, our relationship to God degenerates. We miss the grace of God by it (verse 15). And—as you know—this produces more unholiness, in a vicious circle.

Look how the slide to unholiness is caused. Verse 14; it's by cantankerous, unpeaceful attitudes, stirring, arguing, rather than making every effort for peace. It's by a bitter root (verse 15) that grows and consumes us with hatred, judgement and condemnation. Verse 16: It's sexual immorality. Esau is cited, not because of sexual immorality but because he came to the point of no return, and it is suggesting that those who deliberately go into sexual immorality are actually in danger of going to the point of no return.

So there's a great warning here, to persevere with holiness of life.

With worship (12:18–29)
This is a glorious section! Tom Hewitt in his commentary calls it 'graceful and ingenious'. I think it's marvellous, the great brush-strokes of an artist in a vivid picture of what worship is all about.

The word, in verse 28, for 'worship' is the worship of the sanctuary, *latreuo*, that happens in church and on Sundays. He describes (verses 18–21) what happened in Moses' time, the fear of the mountain.

And, in contrast, he now comes to verse 22. See this as what worship is supposed to be like in your church. 'You have come,' he says…to God, to Jesus. You're not cooped up in a corner, you're part of a vast company, and when you are worshipping together you are locked into heaven. Worship is intended to be the gate of heaven, and in that marvellous phraseology that some of us use in the Anglican Communion service, we say, 'Therefore with angels and archangels and all the company of heaven.' That's exactly this passage—that's where it comes from. We are locked in with all our relatives and friends who have gone before. We're part of a vast company who belong to Him.

It's not the ritual, the place, the form of service or the style of music, but the fact that when we come together, we are to meet with God. It's the expectancy of what He's going to do, the touch of His Spirit upon us, the stirring of our hunger, the marking of us with conviction, the showing us of God and Christ and the Spirit afresh, and the reminding of us (verse 28) that we have a kingdom that cannot be shaken—all will be well! Worship is intended to do all this and so much more.

And that's why we must come reverently, not casually. God forgive us that so often these days, we've treated God like a heavenly chum and not like the living God of the universe. There needs to be reverence. There needs to be the personal relationship, but we need to hold a balance between reverence and awe, and the wonder of being His children. We need to come with prepared hearts. We need to enter the door expecting to meet with God. Everything else is secondary. The holiness (verse 29), like fire, burns up the falsity and shallowness.

Real worship is one of the great strengths to perseverance as Christians.

Concluding exhortation to God's people to persevere (chapter 13)

We come to the last chapter.

I have a feeling that the writer to the Hebrews had a note-pad by his bed to record things he wanted to say to them that he thought of in the middle of the night! He's delivered his soul of all the things he most wanted to say, and in this last chapter he adds the contents of his note-book.

With love (13:1–6)
And love comes first in the fellowship. This is absolutely vital.

Holiness can often make us more judgemental of people. As Christians, we tend to see things more easily in black-and-white terms the closer we come to Christ. That has to be balanced by love that seeks to see the best in

other people. How important that is! If you do get someone in the fellowship who keeps seeing the worst in other
people and refusing to try to see the best, just tread on
them and say, 'The bishop told me to do that!'

And love for strangers—the reference to Abraham.
There's trouble in entertaining, yes, but that's small compared with the blessings. Who are the strangers today?
People away from home, students, overseas students,
away from their country, nowhere to go home for a weekend; nurses, people in the forces, workers in digs. Please
let's be practical as we run through this list.

Love to the suffering—especially in prison. Enormous
trouble was taken to care for Christians in prison, even to
collect much money to pay ransoms. I found this very
moving, and I've checked it and double-checked it. The
early church would say to us, 'The church should collect
money to pay a ransom for Terry Waite.' I know that goes
against all the principles of giving in to terrorists, but
actually this text is speaking about what the early church
did. They loved the person more than the principle in that
case. 'As if you were their fellow-prisoners.' That is real
sympathy.

Who else? The shut-ins, who are elderly and lonely and
sick. How much it means to them to be visited.

Love in marriage, verse 4. We need to say loudly to our
present society that marriage is honourable. Christians are
not to dishonour God by living together sexually without
marrying. Love makes marriage, love should prevent us
turning to adultery and sexual irregularity. As F.F. Bruce
puts it, 'Chastity is not opposed to charity but is part of it,'
and we need to do everything we can to uphold and
support marriage.

Love in values, verses 5–6: not advocating poverty, not
against the enterprise culture, but against a love devoted
to money first.

And notice that it speaks about contentment. We remember Paul's words to Timothy: 'Godliness with contentment is great gain.' And the Christian should be content that the greatest value he or she has, is belonging to God. Verse 5: 'I will never leave you nor forsake you.... The Lord is my helper.' This is the greatest value we should put in life itself. We can sometimes be shocked about immorality but blind to covetousness.

With consideration for and confidence in your leaders (verses 7 and 17)
Most Christian leaders would hesitate to say, as Paul does, 'Be imitators of me.' But we cannot escape it. All of us who are in any position of Christian leadership have a responsibility to seek to make our lives models, if we possibly can, to portray and demonstrate in all our sinfulness and weakness the grace and faith and love of Christ. This is what justifies verse 17; their teaching matters—'who spoke the word of God to you' (verse 7).

But verse 17 can be a charter for authoritarianism, for the sort of shepherding that goes out of control in some house-groups and churches, where people aren't left to think or be answerable to Christ. It's a type of power game. Of course there's a responsibility in leadership, but leadership has to be earned by holiness.

There's concern for leaders here. It's not an easy task—I know it's easy for us leaders to say that, but think of the care, the thought, the sleepless nights of watching, the perseverance, that need to be put into so much of your own leadership. Thinking how better to do it, how to encourage someone, how to discipline someone, how to come alongside someone. And in this the perseverance of fellow Christians helps enormously. Verse 24 says: 'Greet all your leaders', and there's a sense there of love and thought and consideration.

But above all (verse 8), the supreme leader, teacher

and model, the supreme one to obey and submit to is Jesus Christ. We often wrest this passage, this verse, out of its context. 'Jesus Christ is the same yesterday, today and for ever.' But what it's saying is this: however good your Christian leaders are, they come and go. But the one upon whom supremely you should model your life is Jesus Christ, because He is the one whose life and witness of yesterday inspires us, to whom we submit today, in fellowship with Him, and we know He's going to lead the church for ever. He is the supreme leadership model.

With discernment (13:9–10)
Probably the most important need for many Christians today is discernment, among all the strange teachings that surround us.

With courage (13:11–14)
We must be ready to bear His disgrace.

I think of some students, when I was at All Souls, who were converted and went back to their sumptuous homes where their families were upper-class. They were horrified that their daughter or son had become a Christian. Their persecution was horrific—as if they'd become drug addicts. We often have to bear the shame of being outside the camp with Jesus Christ.

With sacrifices (13:15–16)
Perseverance is refreshed and invigorated by giving out to others, and particularly by the sacrifice of praise.

Praise is a great thing for perseverance, isn't it? We've been encouraged by the praise and worship here at Keswick. Also, by witness and action we show the reality of our trust in Jesus.

With prayer (13:18–21)
Apart from the closing greetings of the last verses, there is here a great prayer as the writer arrives at the climax of his teaching about being God's persevering people.

He asks for prayer (verse 18), knowing the pitfalls that face all Christians, not just leaders. How important it is to ask this. Perhaps the words about conscience and intentions suggest there were those distrusting the leaders. But he pervades an atmosphere of trust, and that must be the characteristic of our prayers for anybody.

We need to trust one another more. I wish people would learn that—I wish people who get at me, who actually wrote letters opposing my even being here on this platform, would learn to trust their fellow Christians first. We may disagree with some of the things, but please let's trust one another as brothers and sisters in Christ.

And then comes the great prayer for them, packed with theology enough for a series of studies.

Supremely, it is a prayer that follows from the 'therefore' with which we began this morning. The theology of Christ's shed blood and sacrifice, plus the resurrection (the only place it's mentioned in Hebrews), with practical application to our fulfilling the Chief Shepherd's purposes.

'The God of peace'—there's always peace when we're in the centre of His will. You don't need to be a tense, pushy person—you know some people say, 'I am filled with the Spirit', but they're tense. I say, 'I don't believe you. The fruit of the Spirit is peace.' The God of peace, equipping us to do His will.

And then, matching that as we seek to do His will with His equipment, His divine work in us; 'what is pleasing to him', that wonderful matching of our effort and His power. And His shepherding of us all. What a wonderful prayer it is! An immense encouragement to persevere.

It ends (verse 21) where we must always end, with Jesus Christ. He who has breathed in and through and over this great letter, the Son of God, the Saviour and the King.

Over these mornings we have seen Jesus, who He is. We've fixed our thoughts on how we respond in faithfulness. We've pondered the depths of Jesus and the new covenant and the atonement. And this morning we've fixed our eyes upon Jesus, that we might be truly God's persevering people. And so we acclaim from the heart, in the climax of this prayer, 'Jesus Christ, to whom be glory for ever and ever', Jesus Christ who has the name of all Majesty.

And the letter ends, 'Grace be with you all.'

Maintaining Spiritual Reality

by Mr Charles Price

1. Ritual or Reality?
(1 Samuel 1–3)

It's a great joy to be able to share the Scriptures with you in these morning sessions.

1 Samuel is one of the historical books of the Old Testament, but our primary concern is not going to be history but God; because through the historical record of this book there is a revelation of God that is relevant, practical and significant for us today.

Let me first make a few general comments about 1 Samuel.

It primarily records the transition of Israel from a theocracy to a monarchy. By a theocracy, we mean that God ruled in the nation of Israel ever since they left Egypt and arrived at, and conquered, the land of Canaan. They had no royal family. God had ruled the nation by raising up judges, men and women, through whom He administered the affairs of the nation; and also He led them in their military activities and conquests. But now, having been there for around 250 years, the people are demanding a king. They want their own royal family. Later we'll examine why they demanded this. But this is the main contribution of this book to the Old Testament sequence of historical events.

The story is built around two main characters: Samuel, the last judge, born in chapter 1; and Saul, who became the first king and died in the last chapter of the book. In the shadow of Samuel we find a declining Eli, the last judge but one—and we'll look at him a little this morning; and in the shadow of Saul we find a rising David, anointed king in chapter 16 in private session, set apart by God. David did not actually come to the throne until 2 Samuel, after Saul's death; but Eli at the beginning and David at the end are in the shadows of the two main characters, Samuel and Saul.

Now, in this first study I'm not going to start at chapter 1 verse 1 and work through to the last verse of chapter 3 systematically. I trust I'm going to draw out the main thrust of these chapters, but I think it will be more helpful to us if we pick out various parts to discover the underlying theme that I believe runs through them. And if it all seems a bit of a hotchpotch to you by the end of this morning, well, tomorrow we'll be looking more systematically.

The book opens at a pathetic time in the spiritual life of the nation of Israel. Their spiritual life was centred in Shiloh, which was a town a little over twenty miles north of Jerusalem, some way between Jerusalem and Samaria. When the nation settled in Canaan after the conquest of the country (recorded in the book of Joshua), they set up the tabernacle, the mobile tent in which God had been approached, and where the priesthood functioned. They set it up in Shiloh, and it remained there through the period of the judges, though now, a couple of centuries later, it seems that the tabernacle itself has been replaced by a more permanent structure called in 1 Samuel 'the temple of the Lord'. This must not be confused, of course, with Solomon's temple built in Jerusalem—which he called the 'first temple'—but it was nevertheless a more permanent structure than the original tabernacle.

And when 1 Samuel begins, it's in the hands of a man called Eli, and his two sons Hophni and Phinehas. But things are at a very low ebb.

Chapter 3 verse 1 describes the prevailing spiritual life in Shiloh: 'In those days the word of the Lord was rare; there were not many visions.' In other words, you could gather in Shiloh, but it was very unusual to hear God speak. You might hear the voice of the priest. There was lots of hustle and bustle and activity. But there was never any encounter with God, and people who came to Shiloh left as godless as they may have arrived.

To illustrate that condition and the godless nature of the spiritual life centred there in Shiloh, chapter 1 tells the story of how a man called Elkanah came to Shiloh with his two wives, Peninnah and Hannah, to worship God. 'Peninnah had children, but Hannah had none.' It was a source of great grief to her, and on their annual pilgrimage to Shiloh, she wept and prayed: 'O Lord Almighty, if you will only look upon your servant's misery and remember me, and not forget your servant but give her a son, then I will give him to the Lord for all the days of his life, and no razor will ever be used on his head' (1:9–14). In being given to the Lord, be would be submitted to the Nazarite rules and disciplines.

Hannah stood praying in great anguish (verse 12). She meant business with God. She interceded and asked God to do something in her life—and Eli the priest assumed she was drunk.

Pretty pathetic, wouldn't you say? When a woman does business with God, the priest assumes she's drunk. And if that isn't bad enough, look at chapter 3.

The boy Samuel, born in response to that prayer and taken to Shiloh when weaned, and brought up in the house of the priest Eli, was woken one night by his name being called (3:2–5). 'The lamp of God had not yet gone out'—that's an interesting detail telling us that it was early in the morning. The lamp was lit every night at sunset and burned through the night until dawn broke. So it was near dawn, in the early hours of the morning, and the lamp of God had not yet gone out. And Samuel thought it was Eli calling, 'But Eli said, "I did not call; go back and lie down." '

In other words—'Samuel, go back to bed; you're dreaming!' That happened three times. On the fourth, Eli began to understand; but his first reaction had been that when a boy hears the voice of God, she must be dreaming.

I point it out to you to illustrate the pathetic condition of the spiritual life in Shiloh. No wonder it says, 'The word of the Lord was rare; there were not many visions.'

Eli had been joined in the priesthood by his two sons Hophni and Phinehas. They are described for us in chapter 2—'Eli's sons were wicked men; they had no regard for the Lord' (2:12). They happened to be priests, but they had no regard to the Lord. They could not care less about God, His requirements or His honour. Read verses 13 to 17 of chapter 2, and see something of their operation within the temple in Shiloh; engaging in the priestly duties, they treated the whole proceedings with contempt, demanding the choice pieces of meat that the people brought to sacrifice to God.

There was provision made for the priest from the offerings made in the temple, as we read in Leviticus 7 and Deuteronomy 18. But they were not content with that. In particular, they demanded the fat. The old covenant stated that the fat belonged to God (Leviticus 3:14–16), but these men thought fat was good for them, and demanded it for themselves. Later God condemned them for growing fat on the meat that they'd taken from the offerings that had been presented to God (2:29).

So they've taken it and abused it, and the priesthood has degenerated into just a good occupation with a few perks. As Levites, the job is theirs by right. But now they are exploiting it to their own ends, for their own gratification.

Besides free food there was free sex. They began to exploit and abuse the women who served at the temple (2:22). Of course these were not temple prostitutes such as in Canaanite paganism. They were women ordained to serve the interests of God, but who were perhaps gullible enough to assume that a priest of God was always right. That's a dangerous thing ever to assume about anybody! So when the priests began to take advantage of them and seduce them, they went along with it.

Eli their father should have known better. God spoke to him through Samuel and warned him that 'I would judge his family for ever because of the sin he knew about; his sons made themselves contemptible, and he failed to restrain them' (3:13).

And it seems that Eli had become frightened and intimidated by his own sons and had failed to restrain them, even though he knew of their corrupt practices. In some cases he had even joined in with them, as we can discern from the text.

Now this is the picture of the priesthood. It's either pathetic, in the case of Eli—weak, soft, suspicious; or it's corrupt, in the case of Hophni and Phinehas.

Now having painted that picture from these chapters, I want to ask a very important question: How does the priesthood get into this kind of mess? I have a good reason for asking. What is happening here in 1 Samuel is repeated again and again in history.

You see, no one ever sets out with the intention of being a phoney. No one ever intends to be a hypocrite. No one intends to be unreal with God. When a person comes to Christ, they intend to live in a relationship with God that's real and living and vital. When a person goes into any part of the ministry they do so with the intention that in that ministry they will serve God. But as in this case, something went wrong.

I imagine Eli, as a young man, was thrilled to be called into the ministry. Not every Levite was a priest; it was a particular responsibility and privilege. And I imagine that when God called him he was filled with a sense of privilege, joy, enthusiasm and dedication. And when God broadened his responsibilities and called him to be judge, it must have been because he was a good man. I'm not so sure about his sons. I don't know if they ever had a genuine call from God. But I feel sure Eli did. We only ever see his sons as corrupt men. But somewhere along the line, Eli and his sons lost touch with God. They lost touch with spiritual reality.

I wonder if there's somebody here this morning for whom this may be a true description of their own experience? You remember when God called you to Himself, the sense of joy when you knew that you were forgiven and the Holy Spirit of God had come to live in you, and God now had a plan for you. It's been a long time, a long time since the word of God was fresh to you. It's been rare. No vision, no sense of fresh direction from God.

You will remember the hymn:

Where is the blessedness I knew
When first I saw the Lord?
Where is that soul-refreshing view
Of Jesus through His word?

Are you bored this morning with the Bible, and bored

with God and with your Christianity? If you are, then you might learn some things this morning that will be of tremendous value to you. Because we don't want to just leave Eli and Hophni and Phinehas stewing in their own juice. We want to understand how they got there, and what the way out might have been, though they never took it.

They were priests. That was their function. At the heart of the priesthood lay the responsibility for sacrificial duties. Their primary role was to administer the many offerings and sacrifices. There were two every day. There was the lamb every morning, and the lamb every night. There was sacrifice seven days a week, 365 days a year. There were the sabbath offerings—two more lambs in addition to the daily offerings. On the first day of each month there was the offering of a ram, a goat, seven male lambs, two bulls. There were five annual festivals, some lasting for days, all centring round sacrifices and offerings. I calculate that more than 1,200 animals would be sacrificed annually in Shiloh, as described in Numbers 28 and 29.

And Eli and his sons regularly and consistently fulfilled the duties of these rituals that God ordained. But I want to suggest to you that they had failed to understand the fundamental issue. I think you will be able to draw from their behaviour a logical conclusion: they failed to understand that the value of any ritual is not to be found in the ritual itself, but in the reality of which the ritual speaks and to which it points.

These rituals were symbols. The shedding of blood, the sacrifices, the festivals, the feasts, were not an end in themselves. They were appointed to illustrate two principal realities.

For the worshipper who brought his animal, it was a token of his repentance: 'I am guilty before God. I'm acknowledging my sin. This is a token of my need for cleansing, of my repentance.'

The blood of bulls, goats, rams and lambs never removed sin, it only covered it. I like to understand it as being a little like a post-dated cheque. If you want to make a purchase and you haven't got any money in your bank, you may arrange to give the vendor a cheque post-dated to when you anticipate having money in your account. The cheque has not removed the debt as yet, but it has covered it. It will only remove it when there's money in the bank at the end of the month.

The blood of bulls and goats was like a post-dated cheque, post-dated to Calvary. There was no more virtue in the blood of a bull, a goat, a lamb or a ram than there would be in the blood of any animal. The book of Hebrews makes that very clear. But it was post-dated to Calvary, and when Jesus on the cross declared, 'It is finished', and the curtain in the temple was torn from top to the bottom—the holy of holies now redundant, the priesthood now abolished as no longer necessary—the Lord Jesus was in effect declaring, 'Ladies and gentlemen, there's cash in the bank. Exchange your cheques. Exchange the blood of bulls and goats for the only true currency, the blood of Christ, the precious blood of Christ.' So for the worshipper, it was a token of their repentance.

On the part of God, the blood of the sacrifices was a token of His holiness, justice and need for atonement. But He cannot look at our sin and simply excuse it because He understands it, winking at it and saying, 'That's OK, let's forget it.' It's got to be paid for. And so, as the offerings and the sacrifices were undertaken by the worshipper, it was, on the part of God, an acknowledgement of His holiness. The ritual, the animal brought to sacrifice, was valid as appointed to the reality, the repentance and the holiness of God.

Suppose that people came to Shiloh who ceased to be concerned about this reality. And suppose the priests who handled their offerings also ceased to be concerned about the sin and repentance of the worshipper, about the holiness of God. What do you think would happen?

Well, I'll tell you what I think would—and did—happen. They would still engage in the ritual, but the ritual would replace the reality. The all-important thing would become, not the repentance of the worshipper or the holiness of God, but the sacrifice itself. And one of two things would happen. Either they would eventually desecrate the ritual, saying, 'It doesn't matter any more; we can abuse it, we can play around with it'; or they would deify it and make it into something it is not, a god.

Hophni and Phinehas did both. In chapter 2, they desecrated the ritual, and in chapter 4, as we'll see in another context tomorrow, they deified the ritual. Now, let me bring these principles to bear on our circumstances. We live under the new covenant. It's very, very different to the old one. We're not steeped in rituals as they were. However, there are some symbols that we have been given, and the same problems can happen.

What about the Lord's Supper, the Holy Communion, the Breaking of Bread? You remember—instituted by the Lord Jesus on the night He was arrested, before He was crucified, in that upper room as they were sharing in the Passover meal. The symbol is the bread and wine. The ritual is the eating of the bread and the drinking of the wine. But—'The reality is Me,' said the Lord Jesus. 'This is My body; do it in remembrance of Me. Drink this cup in remembrance of Me.' So the reality behind the ritual is Christ, His death, His shed blood, the reminder of the fact that although we enjoy a free salvation, never, never forget Somebody paid for it, and the price was high.

Now, suppose someone does not know Christ, or that they are a Christian who has ceased to care about the Lord Jesus and His forgiveness, who has ceased to appropriate His death and His shed blood in their lives. Can they still eat of the bread and drink of the wine? Yes, they may; but I'll tell you what will happen. Instead of the ritual pointing to the reality, the ritual will replace the reality, and the all-important thing will become not Christ but it. Have I had *it*? I've heard people speak that way, haven't you? 'I've got to go to Communion, I haven't had *it* for a month.' In due course, instead of remembering Him, thinking of Him, concentrating on Him, they simply are having *it*.

Take that to its extreme and you end up with transubstantiation, holding that the bread becomes the body, the wine becomes the blood.

How about baptism? Another beautiful picture. Now, I must be careful here because we have lots of different views on baptism and I don't want to upset the people who have got it wrong! But consider the view that would see baptism as an identification with Christ and His death, His burial, His resurrection to new life, patterned on Romans 6 (which doesn't actually speak of water baptism, but is a beautiful picture).

So a person goes down into the water—identification with Christ in His death; under the water—identification with His burial; and out of the water—identification with His resurrection, to declare to all who care to see, 'I am now walking in newness of life.'

It's only a picture. The act of baptism doesn't make it happen, it's just a sign, it's a pointer to the reality. It's like a wedding-ring. I have a wedding-ring on my finger. That didn't make me married. If I take it off, I don't cease to be married. It's only a sign. Yet when my wife gave it to me, she made it sound much more. She said, 'With this ring, I thee wed.' I thought to myself, 'Is that all? Just that ring?' What she meant was, it's a sign. It doesn't make me married.

Some people see baptism not as a wedding-ring but more as an engagement-ring. That is, it's a sign in the hope that one day the relationship that it speaks of will be confirmed and made real by that person. Either way, the point is that the ritual is valid insofar as it points to the reality, to our union and identification with Christ in His death and burial and resurrection. If we know nothing of this, the ritual will replace the reality; and the all-important question will be not, 'Am I walking in newness of life?', but 'Have I been *done*?'

I was baptised when I was sixteen. It was announced one day in the church that we attended that in a few weeks' time there'd be a baptismal service. At the end somebody outside the church said to me, 'You're sixteen. Have you ever thought about getting *done*?' Well, as it happened I had thought about getting done. They said to me, 'Why don't you get done with this batch?' So I got done with that batch. No one said to me, 'Do you know what it is to be risen with Christ, to be walking in newness of life—that it's not your life now, it's the life of the risen Christ in you?' I wouldn't have understood that; it would have been a wonderful opportunity for them to have explained it, but no one did. And I got done. Taken to its extreme, a wrong view of baptism leads to baptismal regeneration, where the act of baptism incorporates you into Christ.

What about Bible reading? That's not a ritual in the same way, but Bible reading is vitally important. When someone comes to Christ we usually explain to them, 'It's important that you take time to read your Bible; that's important.' But why? Someone told me I should read my

Bible every day and they didn't tell me why. I wondered why it was so dull, because I began to read my Bible for the purpose of getting to know my Bible. And I discovered that's not the reason for reading the Bible. The reason is to get to know Christ, to get to know God.

We know that, because Jesus criticised some Jews in John 5:39—'You diligently study the Scriptures...' Wouldn't you have thought that would be a commendation? But He continues, in effect, 'You study the Bible to get to know the Bible and it makes you Pharisees; it gives you a set of rules with which you can club people over the head!' The primary purpose of the Scriptures is that through the written word we see the living word and we get to know Christ.

When I got my Nissan car, an instruction book came with it. And I read the instruction book, not because I wanted to know all about the instruction book but for a far more interesting reason. I wanted to know all about the car. Isn't that obvious? I could have read the instruction book, of course, every night before I went to bed. I could have underlined the bits I liked. I could have joined the local Nissan car fellowship. I could have gone every week for an exposition of the manual. This week's subject, Sparking Plugs; next week, a message on Tyre Pressures. I could have put the manual to music and produced a book called *Nissan in Song*. If I were a fanatic, I could study Japanese and read it in the original language.

But I'll tell you something; the day would come when having read my manual every night, underlined it, attended the Nissan Fellowship, put the thing to music and sung it and studied it in Japanese, I would say, 'I'm sick of the manual!' Why? Because the manual has one purpose: to introduce me to the car.

Now, I hope the manual's inerrant. I hope it's true. It's

not divinely inspired, but I hope it's true. But its purpose is to bring me to the car.

And that, you see, is the purpose of the Scriptures. Of course, there are lots of things we learn from them, but primarily it's a revelation of God because you and I were made to be in His image. If you know what God is like you'll understand what you're supposed to be like.

Do you remember that hymn, 'Break Thou the Bread of Life'—'Beyond the sacred page, We seek Thee, Lord'? The Bread of Life isn't the Scriptures. It's Christ. And as we open the book we say, 'Lord Jesus, through these pages we want to see Christ.' That's my prayer for these Old Testament studies, that the end result may be that we know something of Christ, because this is Scripture's supreme purpose.

I mention these things to illustrate, in contemporary Christianity, what was happening in Shiloh. They engaged in all the right rituals, all the right activities, with an increasing level of abuse of them, because they'd lost the reality of God and detached Christianity from God. And, detaching the old covenant regulations from God of whom they primarily spoke, it all became utterly boring. So they had to find their own amusement in the way they handled these sacrifices and handled the people, the women, who served in the temple—purely because they were bored.

Now, what does God do? Well, He sends two messages to Eli. The first comes by an unnamed 'man of God' and is found in 2:27–29.

Did I not clearly reveal myself to your father's house when they were in Egypt under Pharaoh? I chose your father out of all the tribes of Israel to be my priest, to go up to my altar, to burn incense, and to wear an ephod in my presence. I also gave your father's house all the offerings made with fire by the Israelites. Why do you scorn my sacrifice and offering that

I prescribed for my dwelling? Why do you honour your sons
more than me by fattening yourselves on the choice parts of
every offering made by my people Israel?

That's God's summary of what was happening to these
people—called, ordained by God, but corrupted. And
then, in verses 30,31, God says something very frightening:

Far be it from me! Those who honour me I will honour, but
those who despise me will be disdained. The time is coming
when I will cut short your strength and the strength of your
father's house, so that there will not be an old man in your
family line.

If we read on in the rest of that chapter we'll see how
that He tells them of the approaching death of Hophni
and Phinehas, which we'll find in chapter 4 tomorrow.

But do you notice something there in verse 30? God
breaks a promise! Did you know God could break a
promise? What does it mean? Is God untrustworthy? Are
His statements tentative, so that we *hope* He'll honour
them?

No. What we must understand by this, I believe, is that
God is committed to His own agenda; and inasmuch as the
priesthood is part of His agenda, functioning on His terms
and accomplishing His purposes, then it's fine; you'll have
it as long as the priesthood is needed. But if the priests
change the terms and play around with what God has
called them to, then God has not so much broken His
promise as they have stepped out of His purpose.

There's a great verse in 2 Chronicles 15:2, which I came
across recently. It relates to a man called Asa who was on
the throne in Judah, and a prophet called Azariah who
came with a message. Listen to this: 'The Lord is with you
when you are with him.'

And if you think that is an 'Old Testament' principle, there is a verse in the New Testament in which Jesus says: 'Whoever serves me must follow me; and where I am, my servant also will be' (John 12:26). It's the same principle.

I don't know how often you pray, 'Lord, please be with me today.' Do you know something? That is a totally unnecessary prayer. What we need to pray, and what these men ceased to pray in Shiloh, is: 'Lord, help me today, enable me today to be with You, to be in step with You, to be wholly available today to Your purposes, to Your direction, to Your will.' As I am with Him, He is with me. That's the principle.

God's job is not to follow me. Mine is to follow Him, saying, 'Lord Jesus Christ, I want to live my life today in obedience to You, under the direction of Your Holy Spirit and under the lordship of Christ.' And as I do so, I can have absolute confidence that God will be with me. But if I step out of His will and turn my back on His authority, then He will cease to be with me.

The priest was supposed to be where God was, but they had turned their backs on God's purposes, and, as we've already seen, were pursuing their own agendas. And in chapter 3, when God spoke to Samuel that night, when He called him—still only a boy—He let him know a judgement which Samuel then conveyed to Eli the next morning (3:11–18); a judgement on the house of Eli, brought because God is not committed to your programme nor mine if it violates His: His agenda, His purposes.

The sad conclusion to all of this is a statement in Psalm 78, where the psalmist reviews something of the history of the nation of Israel. And he says of God, 'He abandoned the tabernacle of Shiloh, the tent he had set up among men' (Psalm 78:60).

God abandoned it; but—understand this—never before they had first abandoned Him.

Let me tell you something this morning: every one of us here today is as spiritual as we really want to be. Do you understand that? You're as near to God as you have chosen to be. But you side-step, and God is not committed to your side-step. You're on your own. One of the first symptoms of that is that Christianity begins to get boring. The Bible becomes a dull closed book, your prayers hit the ceiling and bounce dead back to the floor.

But there's always, always a way back, as we'll see tomorrow.

One last thing. In all this, what happened to Samuel? As a boy he had been given back to the Lord. That meant he was brought to Shiloh when young. He was growing up in an environment of godlessness. He was with the priesthood, in Shiloh, at the temple of the Lord; but he was having breakfast every morning with Hophni and Phinehas.

The wonder is, 'The boy Samuel continued to grow in stature and in favour with the Lord and with men' (2:26). In other words, he grew physically in stature, spiritually in favour with the Lord and socially in favour with men.

A good environment is helpful. Of course it is. We thank God for any positive, good, helpful, stimulating environment in which we may grow up. But your environment is never the source or secret of spiritual growth. God may be known, loved, served, enjoyed, experienced in the most difficult of environments. That's why on Judgement Day there are no questions about your environment— have you noticed that? The questions are about you. God won't say to you on Judgement Day, 'Which church did you belong to?' He won't respond 'Oh, were you a member of *that* one? Well, it's amazing you're here! Who was your minister? Who was your teacher? Why, you didn't stand a chance!'

He won't ask you that. You'll stand before God alone. Don't blame your environment. I meet people all the time—'If only I could change my church I would be fine spiritually.' It's not true. Your church is not your spiritual life, it's Jesus Christ who is your spiritual life.

So how did Samuel remain in the midst of these circumstances and yet grow in spiritual maturity?

We find his secret in chapter 3, verses 19–21: 'The Lord was with Samuel as he grew up, and he let none of his words fall to the ground.' A great statement that—he never wasted what he had to say. 'And all Israel from Dan to Beersheba recognised that Samuel was attested as a prophet of the Lord. The Lord continued to appear at Shiloh, and there he revealed himself to Samuel through his word.'

Has anybody got a monopoly on His word? No, they haven't. Samuel didn't have the completed word of God that we hold in our hands and call the Bible. But in an environment of spiritual apostasy and barrenness—and more than that, of abuse of the things of God—in the midst of that environment Samuel grew up as a man so that from Dan to Beersheba, from the top to the bottom of the country, they recognised him as someone attested by God because God revealed Himself to Samuel through His word. And it was Samuel's discipline to spend time listening to the word of God.

I want to say to you that if Keswick only gives you a boost for a week you won't have accomplished anything. But if it stimulates you to go back to your home knowing you have in your hands everything God has to say in its entirety, the completed revelation in the Lord Jesus Christ; knowing that you have access to the Lord Jesus Christ through the written word, which reveals to us the living Word; knowing that because our roots go into Him it doesn't matter what your environment may be (though a good one is helpful)—then we will grow.

In the next three studies we'll see Samuel emerging from this background, not with some kind of chip on his shoulder, or a need for some inner manipulation to get him straightened out again, but with a knowledge of God. And we'll see him become God's man in the nation.

I don't know what God, by the Holy Spirit, may have pressed on your heart this morning. My prayer is that as we come as individuals with individual needs and circumstances, that the Holy Spirit may exercise His prerogative of teaching us, personally, things that the person next to us may not even have heard.

Perhaps somebody here is involved in a Christianity where all outwardly appears right; but you know it's become a hollow formality, and deep in your heart you're lonely. When it comes to your knowledge of God, you're probably bored, because the ritualism, the symbols, the practices have replaced the reality. You've lost touch with God.

Then come back! In humility and repentance, be restored again to that relationship where He's your Friend and your Lover, and you love Him.

Is it ritual—or reality?

2. Ichabod or Ebenezer?
(1 Samuel 4–7)

Israel is in combat with the Philistines. The Philistines, as many of you will know, were a ferocious little neighbour on their south-west border. Most of the time the Philistines appear in the Old Testament, they're fighting. We will look a little more at them later, and find out more about why they fought so much and what they were really doing in Canaan, but they've engaged Israel in combat and they have defeated Israel, in the opening verses of chapter 4, and have killed four thousand Israelite soldiers. The Israelites have retreated back to camp with their tail between their legs, and they ask 'Why did the Lord bring defeat upon us today before the Philistines?' (4:3) In other words, 'Where was God when we were in the battle?' Good question.

Then somebody had an idea. 'Let us bring the ark of the Lord's covenant from Shiloh, so that it may go with us and save us from the hands of our enemies' (verse 3).

Now let me explain what lies behind that suggestion. The ark of the covenant was the most important piece of furniture that God told Moses to construct for the tabernacle (you can read the details of its construction in Exodus 25). God had said to Moses, 'There I will meet with you.' And there was the phenomena of the Shekinah glory, present there between the cherubim on top of the ark of the covenant. It was placed in the holy of holies— the most holy place in the tabernacle, called so because God was there. The ark symbolised the presence of God, and He often spoke of it as 'the place where I meet with you'.

The thinking behind verse 3 was this. Although the ark of the covenant was kept in the most holy place, there had been times in its history when it had been brought out of there and taken into a crisis-situation, and God had intervened. Miracles had taken place and enemies had been overcome. The elders of Israel in verse 3, therefore, were relating the military strength of Israel to the carrying of the ark.

Let me remind you of the words quoted in Numbers 10:33–36, spoken by Moses to accompany the carrying of the ark. 'Rise up, O Lord, and may your enemies be scattered; may your foes flee before you.' The carrying of the ark was the symbol of the fact that God was going to fight their battles.

You may remember the clear instructions given to Joshua's army when they came to the Jordan river: 'When you see the ark of the covenant of the Lord your God, and the priests, who are Levites, carrying it, you are to move out from your positions and follow it' (Joshua 3:1–3).

If you read on you'll see that's exactly what happened. 'Joshua said to the priests, "Take up the ark of the covenant and cross over ahead of the people."'... "Tell the priests who carry the ark of the covenant: 'When you reach the edge of the Jordan's waters, go and stand in the river.' "... "And as soon as the priests who carry the ark of the Lord—the Lord of all the earth—set foot in the Jordan, the water flowing downstream will be cut off and stand up in a heap" ' (verses 6,8,13).

And the miracle happened. The waters opened, the people passed through, and then, finally, the people carrying the ark left the Jordan river and the waters began to flow as normal once again. It was the carrying of the ark into the river that precipitated the miracle of the opening of the water.

In Joshua chapter 6, moreover, when they came to Jericho, they were to march around the city once a day for six days, seven times on the seventh day. And they were to carry at the head of the nation the ark of the covenant, and on the seventh day shout for all they were worth. And God performed a miracle; He gave them victory.

That is the background. These Israelites, in the face of their defeat against the Philistines, say, 'Let us bring the ark of the Lord's covenant from Shiloh, so that it may go with us and save us from the hand of our enemies.'

Well, we see what happens in verse 4. We have already met Hophni and Phinehas. Those dirty priests, the sons of Eli, took the ark into battle. The Philistines, seeing them carry the ark, said to each other, 'Be men and fight!', and they thrashed Israel, killed Hophni and Phinehas along with thirty thousand soldiers, and captured the ark of the covenant.

Back in Shiloh, ninety-eight year-old Eli was too old to go to the battle. And his sight was not good, and, it says, he was fat and flabby—'for he was heavy' (verse 18)—we know why: from eating all that choice meat that had been brought to the offerings in Shiloh. As Eli waited in Shiloh, a Benjamite came running back. Eli said, 'What happened?' He gave him the news, and when Eli heard it he fell from his chair, broke his neck, and died.

His daughter-in-law, the wife of Phinehas, was pregnant. When she heard the news she went prematurely into labour, and before she died the last thing she did was to name the baby boy that was born. She called him Ichabod, meaning 'the glory has departed from Israel'.

It's a very tragic story. But I want to suggest to you this morning that the tragedy has its source in a very simple issue. Let me read what Joshua told the people when they took the ark into the Jordan river: 'Consecrate yourselves, for tomorrow the Lord will do amazing things among you' (3:5).

Similarly, in 6:16, circling Jericho for the seventh time on the seventh day, Joshua commanded the people: 'Shout! For the Lord has given you the city!' And in Numbers 10, having gone through the wilderness carrying the ark ahead of the people, they uttered that liturgy, 'Rise up, O Lord! May your enemies be scattered...before you.'

The ark is the symbol of His presence—but it's God, said Joshua, who's going to intervene, who's going to give you the city, who's going to scatter our enemies.

But now, here in 1 Samuel 4:3, what they are saying is: 'Let us bring the ark of the Lord's covenant from Shiloh, so that *it* may go with us and save us from the hand of our enemies.'

The Authorised Version reads: 'Let us fetch the ark of the covenant of the Lord out of Shiloh unto us, that, when it cometh among us it may save us out of the hand of our enemies.' There's a lot of 'it' and 'us' in that verse, isn't there?—very little 'God'. The RSV and the NIV margin have 'He may go with us', but subsequent events confirm that the object of their confidence was not God but the ark. And having detached the ark—the symbol of God's presence amongst them—from God Himself, and put their trust in it, they discovered it was a lifeless box.

Yesterday we saw that when you detach the symbol from its substance, the ritual from its reality, and the symbol—the ritual—replaces the reality, then you either desecrate or deify the ritual. In chapter 2, they desecrated the rituals. Here they deify the symbol.

The mistake they made was this (and this is a lesson of practical value, I believe, for us today). They sought to imitate the pattern of previous victories in the wilderness, in the Jordan, in Jericho; but they had not learned the underlying principle. It is always easier to reproduce a pattern than to apply a principle. And if we reduce the Christian life, or Christian service, to a programme, to a pattern of behaviour that does not require divine initiative and divine activity, we have killed it—as they discovered here.

That is why we do not turn to the Scriptures so much to look for *patterns*; we look for biblical *principles*. You can imitate the pattern and be utterly lifeless; because it's not how God did something in the past, it is *why* God did something, that they needed to understand.

And, you see, it's far easier in our own Christian lives and church lives to try to reproduce patterns that we've seen to work elsewhere, than it is to do dealings with God that are original. Fetch the ark; bring it in the hands of these two wicked priests, Hophni and Phinehas—rather than do business with God Himself, seeking to bring Him into the situation.

Sometimes we hear that revival has broken out in some other part of the world, and we're very excited about it. Often we fly our Christian journalists, strategists and photographers to the scene. They take their pictures; they report what they find; the strategist reduces it to a programme, and puts it into a loose-leaf binder, and comes home and organises seminars on revival—and we wonder why it does not work. It's because we're trying to reproduce the pattern, and God has written across it *Ichabod*; but you can be sure, if revival has broken out somewhere in the world, it has to do with a lot more than just finding the right formula.

Maybe there's a church down the road that's growing, and ours isn't, so we send a few spies over to find out what they do there. And they come back and tell us, 'They've burned their hymn-books. They sing choruses from a big screen.' So we burn our hymn-books. We try to reproduce their pattern. And we wonder, after twelve months, why nothing's happening. So we send the spies back again, and they come back and say, 'We forgot to tell you, they sing them twelve times each!'

I tell you, if God is working, there's a lot more going on than singing songs. And God will write across our attempted imitation, 'Ichabod'.

We learn from other people's programmes—of course we do. But it's not programmes or patterns or the fact that something happened twenty-five years ago that brings about revival; it's the fact that people are in touch with God and He is at work in them. I think that's the reason why revivals and great movements of God rarely live beyond a generation—if that. When God works it is usually because people have been involved in intercession; and through this and other ways, God has begun to work amongst them. And then we reduce it to a formula. It becomes a tradition. And God writes 'Ichabod'.

It can happen in our personal life. I remember, when I was a student in Glasgow at the Bible Training Institute I read the story of C.T. Studd. One of the things C.T. Studd used to do, apparently, was to get up in the middle of the night, pray and read the Bible for an hour, go back to bed and wake up again at the normal time not having missed that hour's sleep at all. I thought, 'That's fantastic! That's the secret of C.T. Studd.'

So I set my alarm for 3.30 the next morning. I got up and made a cup of coffee (it didn't say that C.T. Studd did that, but I needed to) and I knelt down by my bed with my cup of coffee and my Bible and the notebook in which I had prayer items and requests and so on. And I woke up about four hours later with stiff knees and cold coffee. I never tried it again.

I'm sure the angels had a good laugh. 'He thinks the pattern—halfway through the night—is the secret of power.' Nonsense! The secret is of course the fact that C.T. Studd prayed. There's only one true source of power and life and reality, and that is God Himself. We'll discover that when we get to chapter 7.

One of the great things that we learn through Scripture but find hard to learn in practice is that God loves to be original in the way He does things. Have you noticed that?

In Matthew 8 and 9 we have a record of ten distinct miracles that Jesus performed. And if you look at them, you find there's tremendous variety in the ways in which God dealt with the people involved. For instance, the first man who came to Him was a leper. Jesus reached out His hand and touched him and said, 'Be clean.' And he was— he was healed.

Then a centurion came, and said, 'My servant's at home lying sick.' Jesus said, 'I'll come and see him.' And the centurion said, 'No, I don't deserve to have You come under my roof; just say the word and he'll be healed.' Jesus said to the centurion, 'Go! It will be done just as you believed it would.' He didn't see the man, He didn't touch the man, He just spoke the word and away down the road somewhere the centurion's servant was healed.

Some time later a paralytic came, and Jesus didn't touch him but just spoke to him. He said, 'Your sins are forgiven.' Some were upset by that, so He said, 'Which is easier: to say, "Your sins are forgiven", or to say, "Get up and walk"?' But the point is, He just spoke the word to him and he was healed.

A little later a lady in the crowd who had been bleeding for twelve years came and touched the hem of His garment and she was healed as a consequence.

There's tremendous variety in the way that Jesus dealt with these people, which is wonderful. But I imagine it could have caused problems when Jesus left the area. I could imagine some of these people, if they were like we are today, getting together.

'You know, when Jesus was here, He healed me!'

'Well, isn't that wonderful? He healed me too.'

And the first man says, 'You know, when He laid His hands on me, it was as though the power of God was coming through His fingers into my body. I could just feel it surging through my body. Did you feel that when He laid His hands on you?'

And the second man asks, 'What do you mean—laid His hands on me?'

'You mean He didn't lay His hands on you?'

'Well, He just spoke to me. You mean, He didn't speak to you? Didn't you hear that tremendous authority in His voice when He said, "Get up"? Didn't He speak to you like that?'

And the first one says, 'Well, no. But you say He didn't actually touch you? Tell me, are you sure you *were* healed? Are you sure yours wasn't psychological?'

And the second replies, 'Of course my healing is real. In fact, if He had to touch you, I think yours is more likely to be psychological.'

So they probably split up and formed two churches. One would form the Touchy Church. They'd meet every Sunday morning and sing, 'He touched me'. At the end of their service they'd sing, 'To get a touch from the Lord is so real'. Down the road they form the Church of the

Word. They never touch anybody. They sing every Sunday, 'Speak, Lord, in the stillness, While we wait on Thee'.

And then a man moves into the town who's also been healed by Jesus, and they both hear and they both go and knock on his door to invite him to their church. And they arrive together. The man from the Touchy Church says, 'Excuse me, I understand you've been healed by Jesus.'

The man says, 'Yes, I was.'

'Well, that's wonderful; we'd love you to come to our church. Maybe on Sunday night you can give a testimony of how He touched you, how His power came into you.'

And he says, 'Well, actually, that isn't what happened.'

'You mean He didn't touch you?'

So the second man, from the Church of the Word, says, 'Excuse me! Of course He didn't touch you! Would you like to come to our church on Sunday night—we have a great fellowship—and just share how that He spoke the word to you and you just heard that tremendous authority in His voice?'

And the man answers, 'Well, He didn't actually speak to me; I mean, He did speak but that isn't how He healed me.'

'Well, what did He do?'

'Well, He does what He always does when He heals people.'

'What do you mean?'

'Well, He spat in my eye—didn't He spit in yours?'

Incidentally, when you read this story (in Mark 8:22) you find this: 'They came to Bethsaida, and some people brought a blind man and begged Jesus to touch him.' They didn't beg Him to *heal* him. They begged Him to touch him; because 'we've worked out the method, you see, the pattern...Lord Jesus, if You just come and touch him he'll be healed.'

I'd have loved to have been in the crowd, wouldn't you? As the Lord Jesus came alongside the man and stood in front of him, as the crowd waited in stillness—what was He going to do?—He spat in his eye.

So he'll probably form another church called the Church of the Holy Spittle . . .

Next time they brought a blind man to Him they thought they knew the pattern. But He spat and missed, and they thought, 'That wasn't a very good shot.' But He bent over, mixed the spittle into the clay and put it into the man's eye.

Just in case you think you've reduced God to a formula you can reproduce, even though God Himself may not be involved, notice that the important thing in those examples is not how these people were healed, but who healed them.

Never try to reproduce in others what God may have done in you. Don't try to seek some experience in your life that you may have seen God perform in someone else's. Try to push people into your mould, and you'll make them as mouldy as you will become!

I remember speaking in a church in Brisbane, Australia. At the end of the Sunday evening service, a girl asked to talk to me. She said, 'I'm trying to make sense of this Christianity thing.' So we sat down together.

I said to her, 'You'll never make sense of Christianity until you understand Christ, and you'll never understand Christ until you seek after Him.' And I read Matthew 7:7–8 to her, and I told her, 'It's not a matter of understanding doctrine; that isn't the primary thing. It's knowing Christ. And as you seek after Christ you'll find Him.'

The next night we talked again, and she told me, 'You said something to me last night that nobody had said to me before. You told me to seek after God, after Christ.'

I said, 'Yes.'

She said, 'You know, for about two years now I've been trying to make sense of Christianity. I went to one church for several weeks, then I asked the pastor what it means to be a Christian. He said to me, "Well, that's great. Next Sunday night we're having a special evangelistic meeting. You come to that. At the end of the service I'll invite people to walk forward. If you walk forward at the end of that service, somebody will counsel you." So I went to the service, I walked forward, somebody talked to me, but nothing happened in my heart and my life. I went to another church. I told them the same thing and they said, "You're in luck! We just happen to be having a six-week discipleship course every Sunday afternoon starting next Sunday. You attend that course," and I did.'

She said, 'I went through those six Sunday afternoons, and at the end of six weeks they said, "Now, some of you may want to become members of the church and if you do, then this is what you should do."

'I went away,' she said, 'and I thought, "Well, I haven't found what I'm looking for." Then I went to another church, and I told them, "I don't understand the Christian life and I want to." They took me into a room where about four of them put their hands on me and prayed for me—and they really prayed for me,' she said. 'But nothing happened.'

She said, 'I've been searching for two years. Nobody ever said to me, "Seek for God." '

Isn't that tragic? There's nothing wrong in going forward; nothing wrong in going on a discipleship course, I'm sure that was helpful to her; nothing wrong in someone laying their hands on her and praying for her—except that none of those things are the issue.

This is what's happening in 1 Samuel 4. They were godless men, Hophni and Phinehas who brought the ark.

We saw them yesterday. 'Let's get the technique right; bring the ark, follow the pattern'—and the result is they're left with baby Ichabod, the only line in that priestly family of Eli still alive, as far as we know.

Well, what happened next? Let me take you through chapters 5 and 6 very quickly.

The Philistines decided to pay due homage to the Israelite God; they put the ark in the temple of Dagon. Soon the statue of Dagon was fallen and broken, and they said (verse 7): 'The ark of the God of Israel must not stay here with us, because his hand is heavy upon us and upon Dagon our god.' They sent the ark to Gath, and when it got there, tumours broke out in that city. So they sent it to Ekron. And they passed the ark around Philistine territory like a hot potato for seven months.

God honoured amongst pagans what He refused to honour amongst His own people who should have known better. You see, it was the ark of God. It was the place where God said, 'I'll meet with you.' It was the symbol of His presence. Amongst pagans who did not know better they felt the brunt of His presence.

And so, in chapter 6, the Philistines called for the priests and the diviners and said, 'What shall we do with the ark of the Lord? Tell us how we should send it back to its place.'

They put the ark of the covenant on to the cart, hitched at least two cows, and sure enough the cows headed straight for Israel with the Philistines following behind it until it came to the border, to a town called Beth Shemesh. There the Israelite people were harvesting their wheat, and they saw the ark arriving on the back of the cart. They were so excited. They took the ark off the cart. They chopped up the cart, made a fire and offered the cows as a burnt offering to God.

Then some of them looked into the ark. 'God struck down some of the men of Beth Shemesh, putting seventy of them to death because they had looked into the ark of the Lord' (6:19). Some manuscripts say 'fifty thousand-and-seventy', but it's more likely to be seventy in view of the size of Beth Shemesh.

They looked into the ark—they'd been told not to do that—and they discovered something. If you approach God other than on the basis of shed blood, you find Him not to be a Friend, you find Him to be a Judge. God severely chastised them; seventy of them died.

So they took the ark through to Kiriath Jearim. 'The men of Kiriath Jearim came and took up the ark of the Lord. They took it to Abinadab's house on the hill and consecrated Eleazar his son to guard the ark of the Lord. It was a long time, twenty years in all, that the ark remained at Kiriath Jearim' (7:1–2).

I want you to notice, there's going to be a totally different atmosphere in chapter 7 to that in chapter 4. 'All the people of Israel mourned and sought after the Lord' (7:2). Before, they placed their confidence in *it*, in the ark; 'It will save us.' Now, chastised, beaten, humiliated, having had time to draw their breath and ask the important question, 'What went wrong?', they are now seeking after the Lord.

Notice the difference in the language in verse 3. It's He who 'will deliver you'. And Samuel says to them, 'If you're returning to the Lord, if you're coming back to God, then get rid of all these other objects of dependency, these Ashtoreths, these foreign gods.'

Incidentally, though it says that they put away their Baals and their Ashtoreths (verse 4), the foreign gods may not necessarily be just pagan deities. Their confidence was in God Himself, and they would have turned away from any other dependency, even on things God-ordained and good. Do you remember the account of Hezekiah in 2 Kings 18:2? He was a good king: 'He did what was right in the eyes of the Lord, just as his father David had done. He removed the high places, smashed the sacred stones and cut down the Asherah poles.'

We would have cheered him on, wouldn't we? But look at how the verse continues: 'He broke into pieces the bronze snake Moses had made.' Do you remember the bronze snake? In the wilderness, God told Moses to make it and put it on a pole; anybody bitten by a snake could look at it and live. In John 3:14 we're told it's a picture of Jesus. Hezekiah, the good, godly king came to the throne, and broke it: why? 'For up to that time the Israelites had been burning incense to it.' They had taken what was God-ordained, a picture of Christ, and they offered incense to it. And God said to godly Hezekiah, 'Smash it to pieces!'

I wonder what objects of dependency there are, other than God, in your life? What are you depending on for your spiritual growth and vitality? You've come to Keswick to accumulate more information? Well, of course, information's important. We're transformed by renewing our minds. But, as we suggested yesterday morning, that information—the purpose of Scripture—is to lead us to Christ, to God. He is the object on which we're depending. He is the one who alone can bring spiritual vitality and reality and power into our lives.

Sometimes God has to strip us of our spiritual taboos, until we're left only with Him. That's why God told Paul He would not take his thorn out of the flesh. He derived no joy from Paul's thorn. He does not have a morbid sense of satisfaction in our suffering. But He said to Paul, in effect, in 2 Corinthians 12, 'Paul, this is good for you, because the weaker you are, the more your dependency will be on Me, and therefore the stronger you'll be where it really matters.'

In 7:3 comes the promise: having told the people to get rid of the foreign gods, Samuel says, 'He will deliver you out of the hand of the Philistines.'

It's not some programme to work through. Please don't misunderstand me. Of course, they needed a strategy for battle. They would need commanders and leaders, back-up troops. But—'It's God who'll deliver you from the Philistines.'

In verse 7, the Israelites are afraid because of the Philistines. With good reason—their history was one of being defeated by them. But they say to Samuel—note this—'Do not stop crying out to the Lord our God for us, that he may rescue us from the hand of the Philistines.'

So, though afraid of these Philistines, they go in saying, 'Samuel, cry out to God that He'll intervene.' And He does. 'Then Samuel took a sucking lamb and offered it up as a whole burnt offering to the Lord. He cried out to the Lord on Israel's behalf, and the Lord answered him.' God thundered and the Philistines were defeated. And, in verse 12: 'Samuel took a stone and set it up between Mizpah and Shen. He named it Ebenezer, saying, "Thus far has the Lord helped us." So the Philistines were subdued and did not invade Israelite territory again.'

We've had two Hebrew words this morning. In chapter 4, the word *Ichabod*: 'The glory has departed from Israel'; in chapter 7, the word *Ebenezer*: 'Thus far has the Lord helped us'—'We don't congratulate ourselves on our tactics and strategy [though they had to think about those things]. It's God who gave us the victory. He helped us.'

I want to ask you this morning—because it's so important that as we study the Scriptures we apply their principles to our hearts and lives—which of those two words more accurately describes your experience? *Ichabod*: the glory departed, no power, no sense of divine activity in and through your own life, though you're doing all the right things? Or is it *Ebenezer*: God helps me, God is at work?

We can't answer that question by looking for results. Jeremiah preached for forty years and never saw a convert. He had a melancholic temperament, he probably got depressed. If he'd been here this morning, he probably would have said, 'I'm Ichabod.' He never saw results. When he died, of course, he left behind his scroll, which became one of the longest books in the Bible. God was at work through him.

To answer the question, we need to ask another: 'What are you relying on for your effectiveness?'

I trust you want to be effective, that your Christianity is not merely a ticket to heaven. I trust you have in your heart a hunger that one day you will be able to say, 'Here on earth my life has a cutting edge for God'; because He has plans for every one of us.

What are you relying on? Is it God Himself? Is He the one you go to every new day, saying, 'Father, today I acknowledge my own weakness; it is only by Your Holy Spirit in me today that I can be effective and strong and godly and fruitful, and the fruit of the Spirit may be evident in my life'?

Or are you relying on some technique, or on some experience that increasingly recedes into your past so that you're trying to recreate it?

How about Christian service? God called you to teach a Sunday school class, to witness to your neighbours, to lead a Bible class, to lead a youth group, to lead a women's meeting, to preach, maybe in full-time ministry? What are your credentials? Is it that God called you, that you know in your heart that God put you there, and that He who calls you is faithful—He will do it, as you live in that disposition of trust.

Or do you think your education is what will make you effective? 'If only I get three years of Bible training, that will make me effective.' Well, it will give you more information; but it won't make you more effective in itself.

Maybe you're relying on your God-given gift.

As these people went, in chapter 4, they relied on something God-ordained and God-initiated, but it was not God they relied on, it was the *it*. You dare to stand to preach, confident that 'God gave me the gift of preaching'—and your words will bounce off the walls and drop dead on the floor, and nobody will be saved and nobody will be blessed. So as you stand to preach you say, 'God, You alone are the one who can penetrate people's hearts and make Jesus Lord in their understanding.' That's why, of course, you can preach with confidence, teach a Sunday school class with confidence, witness to your neighbour with confidence—if it's God, if it's Ebenezer that you're looking to.

I finished yesterday morning with a question, 'Is it ritual or reality?' I finish this morning with a question: Is it Ichabod or is it Ebenezer?

3. Cowardice or Confidence?
(1 Samuel 8–31)

We are going to look at the life of Saul a little bit this morning. Tomorrow we'll concentrate on just one aspect of his reign, but today we'll look at the whole story.

An important transition is taking place at this stage in the political life of Israel. Ever since they arrived in Canaan, Israel was a theocracy. It was God's prerogative to raise up men and women to lead the nation. We call them judges; they administered the affairs of the people and led them in their military activities. But there was no relationship between one judge and the next. Although the people recognised those whom God had called, the initiative and the prerogative belonged to God, often with some divine revelation that He made to the chosen individual. You see that happening in the book of Judges.

But now, after about two-and-a-half centuries, they want to be a monarchy. They want their own royal family, they want little princes to admire and watch grow up just as we do in Britain.

There were two basic reasons for this on Israel's part. One was a sad reason and the other a bad one. We find the sad one in the first five verses of chapter 8: Samuel in his old age, we're told, appointed his sons Joel and Abijah as

judges for Israel. He had no right to do so. No judge
appointed his successor, and certainly not his own sons to
keep the position within the family. But sad as that aspect
may be, his own sons, it says, did not walk in the ways of
God. They took bribes, they were dishonest and they
perverted justice.

I think it's very sad that the sons of a godly man like
Samuel did not follow in his ways. We can never guarantee the spiritual lives of our children. You do not inherit
spiritual reality.

There's a statement in Proverbs which says, 'Train a
child in the way he should go; when he is old he will not
depart from it.' But understand it correctly. It is not a
promise. It's a proverb. A proverb is a general statement
of principle—'You bring up a child in the way he should
go and he won't depart from it.' But Proverbs also tells us
that a man may have a fool for a son.

Samuel could not guarantee the godliness of his own
children. It caused the desire for a king. They said, 'We
don't want these godless sons of yours, Samuel, to reign
and exercise this authority within the nation.' And that
was the first reason; his sons turned away from the ways of
Samuel (8:5).

Samuel warned people what would happen if they had a
king. But then (verse 19) the people refused to listen to
him. 'We want a king over us. Then we shall be like all the
other nations, with a king to lead us and to go out before
us and fight our battles.' And that was the second reason,
the bad one.

The international and inter-tribal peer pressure was
wearing them down. We do not like being unique; we
want to be like everybody else. But that's a bad reason to
do anything, especially amongst the people of God.

These two reasons fuelled the desire for a king, and so

God gave them one (verse 21); His choice is recorded in chapter 9. God chose Saul.

I want to talk a little this morning about Saul's life, and then we're going to make some applications and learn some lessons.

He is introduced in 9:2 as being impressive, without equal, a head-and-shoulders above the rest of his contemporaries. In the following verses we have the story of Saul's father, Kish, losing some donkeys and sending Saul with a servant to find them. They looked all day, high and low, over a vast territory, and still couldn't find them. And then (verse 6) the servant suggested they consult the 'man of God', who was Samuel, the first of the prophets as he is often called. So they went to ask Samuel to help them find the donkeys. And it happened that God had revealed to Samuel that Saul was going to be the king (verses 15–17).

The Lord makes a particular statement about what Saul's reign will involve—the release of Israel from the Philistines—and we're going to come back to that in just a moment. But let me take you ahead first to 10:1 to see what happened. 'Samuel took a flask of oil and poured it on Saul's head and kissed him, saying, "Has not the Lord anointed you leader over his inheritance?" '

So in a private ceremony Samuel anointed Saul, and gave him several signs that would confirm to him that this was of God. Then, verse 9, 'As Saul turned to leave Samuel, God changed Saul's heart.'

I point you to these verses quite deliberately. I want you to see there was divine activity in the experience of Saul at the beginning of his reign. At Gibeah he joined the procession of prophets and the Spirit of God came upon him and he joined in their prophesying (verses 10–11). And the rumour-mongers, the gossipers, spread the word around: 'Something's happened to Saul! God is on him!

The Spirit of God is working in him!' It's important that you understand this.

Then he was presented publicly to the people. Saul was very fearful and shy. He hid amongst the baggage. But (verse 23) he was brought out to the people who shouted 'Long live the king!' Samuel explained to them the regulations of the kingship. He wrote them down on a scroll and deposited it before the Lord. Then Samuel dismissed the people, each to his own home.

Saul too went to his home in Gibeah, accompanied by valiant men whose hearts God had touched. But some trouble-makers said, 'How can this fellow save us?' They despised him and brought him no gifts. But Saul kept silent.

The people were not unanimous in their approval of his kingship. But then, in chapter 11, we have his first assignment. This is important background to what we will discover about Saul. An Ammonite named Nahash besieged Jabesh Gilead, which was one of the towns in the Jordan valley, on the east side, in actual fact, of the river, and they humiliated the people. And news of this reached Saul. He burned with anger, and as a result of his response (11:6–7) 'the terror of the Lord fell on the people, and they turned out as one man'. They went to fight, and released the people of Jabesh Gilead, and (verses 14–15) Saul was reaffirmed as king with 'a great celebration'.

No record now of the hesitancy of those in chapter 10 who weren't sure that Saul was right! He's proved himself, by God coming upon him and equipping him with power, making him angry and motivating him to go out and release the people of Jabesh Gilead.

Now, so far we've established several things about Saul. God has chosen him. God has called him to the throne (chapter 9). God has changed Saul's heart (chapter 10). The Holy Spirit has come upon him in power (chapter

10). Saul has proved himself as a military leader, as a man able to mobilise and lead the people effectively into battle (chapter 11). So far so good. Here's a man God has called, God has equipped, God has used.

But the story of Saul is a tragic one, because it is a story not of success but of failure; not of victory but of defeat. It's not a story in which the people of Israel could take pride, but one about which they would be embarrassed. And I want this morning to try to understand with you Saul's failure; and maybe as we look into the word of God we'll discover ourselves looking into a mirror. The Scriptures are a very remarkable kind of mirror. They don't just show us what we are and leave us helpless and humiliated by our failure, but they also show us the kind of person that God intends us to be—and, more than that, the resources by which He will make us what He wants us to be.

And I know in my own heart, you can't teach the word of God without either becoming hardened to the Spirit of God or being driven back again and again in humility and repentance, because of our own failure and all the seeds that lie latent in my heart and your heart. In Saul's heart those seeds were allowed to grow, and to become the root that if ignored will begin to bear fruit.

The best way, it seems to me, to understand Saul's failure is against the background of the only promise—so far as I can see—that God made about the reign of Saul. We find it in 9:15–16: 'He will deliver my people from the hand of the Philistines.'

Let me tell you a little about the Philistines. We met them in chapters 4 and 7. They were the major thorn in the flesh of Israel at this stage, and I'll tell you why. They were not native to the land of Canaan. They were not amongst the tribes that Joshua was told to drive out when they came into Canaan. The Philistines originally came from Asia Minor, migrating across the Mediterranean, spending time in Crete but moving on later to the north coast of Egypt. And when Israel left Egypt at the time of the Exodus, they were then along the coastal route between Egypt, up as far possibly as Gaza, so much so that Israel had to detour to avoid unnecessary conflict with them.

But after they had settled in the land of Canaan, the Philistines began to nudge a little more up the coast, and by the time Joshua was an old man (Joshua 13) he told the people that they would have to fight them after all.

During the book of Judges they were the major enemy that Israel was fighting against. And the reason for this would seem to me to be fairly obvious. The Philistines, a later arrival in that area than the Israelites to whom God had given the land, were intent on taking the land for themselves. So they were no ordinary enemies of Israel. They had a subversive intention; to rout Israel out of Canaan, the land God had given them and promised would be theirs for every generation.

So it's not just a territorial skirmish; the Philistines' territory was acknowledged and recognised. But they are aggressive and are therefore a major enemy, not only against the people of God, but against the purpose of God. And when anybody rises up, as the Philistines had done, against God's purpose for His people in Canaan, then they automatically declare themselves God's enemies.

And the primary role that God has declared for Saul at the outset, before he was crowned, is that 'he will deliver my people from the hand of the Philistines'. That statement is clear and unambiguous. You cannot read it to mean something else. And yet the tragedy is, it never happened.

There was plenty of opportunity for it, because 'All the days of Saul there was bitter war with the Philistines, and whenever Saul saw a mighty or brave man, he took him into his service' (4:52). It wasn't because Saul was short of men, but all through his life there was bitter war, and he was on the throne for forty years at least (cf. 13:1).

Saul's death is recorded in chapter 31, in dangerous circumstances, on Mount Gilboa; many were killed with him. Saul's son (and David's great friend) Jonathan, about whom we have no time to speak in these studies, died there with his two brothers. Saul died by his own hand, with his three sons and the armour-bearer who was too frightened to slay his king at his own request.

They were fighting the Philistines on Mount Gilboa, more than forty years after God made a promise to Saul to deliver Israel from them. When the Philistines arrived victorious at the scene, they cut off Paul's head. They stripped him of his armour and hung it up in the temple of their pagan idols. This is the man God had called—and they're putting his armour in a pagan temple, next to their pagan idols. His body they hung on the wall in Beth Shan to exhibit the fact that they had beaten God's king of Israel.

It's a tragic story, especially in view of that forty-year-old promise. It was never fulfilled. Why?

I believe it's very important to understand why, because we'll discover, as we do through Scripture, a principle that may apply in your life this morning. There are promises God has made that you've read in His word. You've underlined them, memorised them, stuck them on a wall maybe as a reminder. But they've never worked out in your experience.

I remember a woman in her early twenties coming to me after a meeting in Scotland. She opened her Bible to 2

Corinthians 5:17, 'If any man is in Christ he is a new creation; old things are passed away, all things are become new.' The verse was crossed out in thick black biro. She said, 'It's not true. I've been a Christian for two years and to call me a new creation is a gross exaggeration. To say old things are gone isn't true. Nothing's gone! To say all things are become new is just not true!'

Why is it that God can declare things in His word that are never anywhere near confirmed in our own experience? Why is it so many Christians live in perpetual weakness, when God has promised power? Why is it that so many Christians can be so unkind, when Jesus said the hallmark of being a Christian is that we have love? Why is it that so often we're defeated again and again in the same areas, when Scripture says, 'Sin will not be your master'? Why is it that again and again God says things and they don't work? This is Saul's testimony.

To understand it, I want to look at how Saul fought the Philistines, because the promise was made specifically concerning his conflict with them.

We have the record of three battles with the Philistines in 1 Samuel.

Firstly, the battle in Geba, a town down in the south that had been captured by the Philistines, though it was a long way from their borders. That battle is described in chapters 13–14. Then in chapter 17 there's a battle in the Valley of Elah, where Goliath appeared; and in chapters 28–31, there is the battle on Mount Gilboa, which is in the far north of Israel.

Now we'll look briefly at these three battles, and in each of them you will find there is a consistent characteristic of Saul. Let me point it out to you. At Geba, Saul and his troops were 'quaking with fear' (13:7). At the Valley of Elah, after Goliath uttered his challenge, 'Saul and all the Israelites were dismayed and terrified' (17:11). Go to chapter 28, to the battle on Mount Gilboa, the battle in which Saul lost his life. 'When Saul saw the Philistine army, he was afraid; terror filled his heart' (verse 5).

Now, what is fear? Well, I suggest to you that fear is primarily an emotion that we feel when we're faced with a threat bigger and more powerful than ourselves or our resources. In those circumstances, I'm afraid.

If I can give you an illustration, just to lighten things for a moment, I think one of the occasions I've been most afraid in my life was when, several years ago, I was visiting South India as a speaker at a conference that was held in the Nilgiri Hills at a beautiful conference centre in what they call the largest game reserve in the world. It's not a fenced reserve, it's simply a protected area where the animals are free to roam. There are houses and even towns in the area. But they have lots of wild animals around, especially elephant; they are famous for their elephant.

The night I arrived we were woken up at three o'clock in the morning because an elephant had come on to the property. (Apparently one night a week before, another had come and scratched itself on the conference hall, and the conference hall had fallen down. It had taken them all next morning to put it back up again—which shows you what kind of conference hall it was!) They woke us up to go out and chase this elephant off the property, which was great fun. I have a farming background, and I thought all you did was pick up a stick, hit the elephant on the backside and say, 'Go on, shoo!'

But they pulled me back. 'Don't get close. It will turn round, pick you up, toss you in the air, catch you on its tusk, put you on the ground, turn around and sit on you! And you won't be very comfortable afterwards.' They told me stories of naïve visitors who had been treated that way. So we just threw stones and made noises and hoped the elephant would move in the right direction, which it did; and we went back to bed.

But a couple of days later that week, I went for a walk on my own along one of the jungle paths by a river. I turned a corner between banks of thick undergrowth, and coming towards me was a huge elephant. When it saw me, its ears went out and its trunk came up. Now, I'd been told that was a danger sign. I think my heart stopped beating. I stood frozen to the spot for what seemed a long time. Then, purely instinctively, I leapt into the river.

It wasn't very wide. When I landed, I remembered there were crocodiles in the river! As I climbed out of the water, I looked behind. My leap into the river had so frightened the elephant that it was now running off in the other direction, smashing branches on either side of the path in its haste.

When they heard my story, the Indian folks gave me a nickname which means 'The One of Whom Elephants Are Afraid'. During that visit I was asked to preach at a place a hundred miles away, and I was introduced as 'The One of Whom the Elephants Are Afraid', and they all sat very quietly and listened. So it was a quite useful title!

But I don't know about the elephant being afraid, I was scared stiff. Now why was I scared stiff? For a very simple reason: I was faced with that elephant, and I had been told what an elephant could do to me. I couldn't fight back; it was bigger than me. So my natural reaction was fear.

Last year, I met another wild animal. I and a friend tried to catch a mouse in his home. We had fun for half an hour trying, and eventually we caught it and put it outdoors. We weren't scared of it.

Why not? It was a wild animal, and in some circumstances it might have been dangerous. But I was scared of the elephant and not of the mouse. Why? Because the elephant was bigger than me, the mouse was smaller than me.

I tell you this for a simple reason.

Why was Saul scared of the Philistines? For a fairly obvious human reason. Turn to chapter 13 again, and I'll show you why Saul was afraid. He chose three thousand men from Israel (verse 2). That was his army: keep that figure in mind. Now look at verse 5: 'The Philistines assembled to fight Israel, with three thousand chariots, six thousand charioteers, and soldiers as numerous as the sand on the seashore.' The AV says thirty thousand chariots. The NIV's three thousand is more likely to be correct, but there's clearly ambiguity in some of the earlier manuscripts. I imagine Saul prefers the New International Version.

The point is this: he counted his men, and he counted theirs, and he came to an obvious conclusion—'We can't beat them.' That's obvious, isn't it? Well, humanly speaking. The fact that God had made a promise was totally irrelevant in practice to Saul. It made no difference to his reckoning.

Now, you may say, 'Well, the promise wasn't made to Saul, it was made to Samuel about Saul, and maybe Samuel didn't tell him; maybe he didn't know this was his brief.'

Well, I feel quite sure that Samuel would have told Saul that, but there's no record of him doing so. However, I'll tell you what Saul was told. Go back to chapter 10, verses 6 and 7. 'The Spirit of the Lord will come upon you in power, and you will prophesy with them; and you will be changed into a different person. Once these signs are fulfilled, do whatever your hand finds to do, for God is with you.'

We have seen that the Spirit of God did come upon

Saul. He'd been called by God, he'd had experience of
God; but in his own reckoning the only resources he had
were his own ingenuity, his own tactics. And, despite the
promise of God, he was living by his own wits and
resources.

Do you remember that lovely incident in John 6, when
Jesus fed the five thousand? Jesus said to Philip—and I
think it's a lovely illustration of what we're talking
about—'Where shall we buy bread for these people to
eat?' (verse 5). I like the next verse, don't you? 'He asked
this only to test him, for he already had in mind what he
was going to do.'

He wasn't stumped, He wasn't looking for advice, He
wasn't saying, 'Philip, I don't know what to do; give me
some ideas.' He knew what He would do. But He wanted
to test Philip. How did Philip respond? Well, he
answered, 'Eight months' wages'—or, in some translations, two hundred denarii—'would not buy enough
bread for each one to have a bite!' In other words, Philip
said to the disciples, 'How much money have we got?
Where's Judas? Judas, how much is in the bag? Two
hundred denarii? Is that all? Man, that's hopeless.' He
came back and said, 'Two hundred denarii would not be
enough; we can't do it.' That's Philip.

Supposing Jesus had called an atheist out of the crowd
instead and asked him the questions. How do you think
the atheist would respond? Well, I suggest to you that he
would have given an identical answer to the one Philip
gave. I'd describe Philip at this stage as a professing Christian but a practising atheist. When it came to facing crises,
when it came to facing difficulties, he had no resources
that the pagan atheists did not have.

That was Saul, too. Not a Christian, of course, but a
man God-ordained, yet living like an atheist. And as we
turn to chapter 17—what difference does it make that

Christ lives in *you*? How does it make your approach to problems and crises different to that of your neighbour faced with the same problems and crises?

In chapter 13, the numerical strength of the Philistines frightened him. In chapter 17 it was a different problem; the enormous size of a single man. They were in the valley of Elah, lined up for battle, when a tall Philistine stepped out with a novel proposal. You know the story. Goliath said, in effect, 'Instead of having all you Israelites fighting all us Philistines, and every night burying our dead until one day we come to some conclusion and somebody wins the battle—why don't we have one Philistine fight one Israelite, to decide the whole war? If the Philistine wins, then we'll tell you what to do; if the Israelite wins we'll be your servants.'

A novel proposal, don't you think? That would be like, back in the days of the Cold War (which we trust have gone), proposing to settle the tensions between America and the Soviet Union by putting a champion of each side in a boxing-ring and agreeing to be bound by the result of the fight.

That was the proposal, and for some reason Saul accepted it; I don't know why.

And then the challenger introduced himself. Goliath was over nine feet tall—he's even mentioned in *The Guinness Book of Records* (he's mentioned in the margin, because his height can't be verified...). There is some ambiguity in the texts. The Septuagint version puts him at about six-and-a-half feet. But he was probably over nine feet.

Having made the challenge, he announces himself as the Philistine's champion (17:4). Read the description of him in verses 4–7. Just the iron point of his spear weighed about fifteen pounds! And this big man with his heavy

uniform puts out the challenge: 'I am fighting for the
Philistines; who's fighting for you?'

There was one obvious choice: Saul. For two reasons:
One, he was head-and-shoulders above all the others. He
could at least look Goliath in the navel. Two, God had
declared His purpose to Saul, 'He'll deliver Israel from
the Philistines.' Samuel had instructed him, 'Find what
there is to do and do it, and God will intervene. He's with
you.' But instead his reaction was, 'Saul and all the
Israelites were dismayed and terrified' (verse 11). And
every day for forty days, Goliath stood out of the camp
and said, 'Where's your man?'

Saul looked for a volunteer; there weren't any. He tried
to bribe them: 'If anybody goes and fights him you can
have great wealth.' That may have sounded attractive
until you stopped to think about it. What happens if you
lose? You can always have an expensive funeral, but that
isn't most people's idea of living.

'Not only will you have great wealth, you can have my
daughter in marriage' was a second proposal. We don't
know whether that was an attractive proposition or not,
but nobody took it up.

'Not only great wealth and my daughter in marriage—
but the whole of your father's family will be free from tax
for the rest of their days.' Now, I imagine all kinds of
people pricked up their ears. They probably got hold of
the weed of the family; 'You won't win, but at least we'll
be tax free—off you go!'

But after forty days there were no takers, and a boy called
David came on to the scene. Too young to be a soldier,
left at home to look after his father's sheep while his
brothers were in the army, and he was sent with bread and
cheese and barley. He came on the scene and said (I'm

paraphrasing): 'Why aren't you fighting?' And the soldiers and his brothers told him about Goliath.

David asked, and again I'm paraphrasing, 'But isn't God on your side?'

They probably said, 'David, don't be so spiritual.'

People say that now; they probably said it then. 'You've got to be realistic about these things; you've got to be practical.' Well, of course you have. But your dependency is not your practicality. That's why they were scared, because they had no one to match him. Their dependency should have been on God. And his brothers were angry and said, 'Don't come here and humiliate us, talking that kind of nonsense.' And they kicked him out and told him to go home.

He didn't. He was sent for by Saul, and had the same conversation with him. 'Well, it's like this, David, this man is a big giant, he's very well equipped, he's experienced, he's already known as a champion; he's put out this challenge.'

'But isn't God on your side?'

'David, it's lovely to hear the enthusiasm of young people, but you'll get out of it; you'll grow out of it!'

Fortunately, David didn't. Don't let anyone make you grow out of a reckless God-confidence! Reckless in the sense, not of being irresponsible, but reckless in that when God says something you believe it although the whole world would seem to contradict it.

And David said a very important thing to Saul. He told him about his exploits killing lions and bears in defence of his sheep, and added: 'The Lord who delivered me from the paw of the lion and the paw of the bear will deliver me from the hand of this Philistine' (verse 37).

Do you see what David's saying there? He's saying, 'Saul, I have already proved God in lesser circumstances than this. Once out looking after my father's sheep, a lion came and a bear came. And I reasoned this way: if God called me to be a shepherd, he called me to be a good shepherd. And if God called me to be a good shepherd, God will enable me to be a good shepherd.'

(By the way, don't relegate God's activity just to 'Christian' work and spiritual activity. God will be God in your office, in your school, in your college, in your home, in your football field, wherever you are.)

David said, 'I've proved God. I went after the bear, took it by its beard and slew it; took the lion, took the sheep from its mouth and slew it.' When I say these were lesser circumstances, I don't mean they were easier circumstances. I personally might rather have taken on the giant than take on a lion. I think they were made of different stuff in those days. I like the way it's said of Samson, he tore a lion apart with his bare hands 'as he might have torn a young goat' (Judges 14:6).

Oh yes, David was a man's man. But he's saying, 'In lesser circumstances, I've proved God.' You see, if I was David's father, I would probably have said, 'David, I hope you didn't try and fight that lion; I hope you came back with the other sheep safe.' But David was wise enough to know that a lion is like a fox: if it takes a sheep today, it'll be back tomorrow and the next day; it'll come back every day that a sheep is there to be taken.

David is saying, 'I've proved God on the hills around Bethlehem when nobody was looking, and therefore I have a history and a memory of a God who works.'

Do you know why some of us fall flat on our face when we face the big issues? Because we have never proved God in the little issues, when nobody's looking. So we've compromised in our office, our school, our home, our place of work, our family life. And we have no history, no memory of God intervening to meet our needs. And many of us are powerless in the big things who have never proved Him in the little things. Let me tell you, you'll never leap-frog into spiritual maturity.

There are crises in the Christian life. Many of us look back on events of which we remember the date and time, but they are not normally the most important events in our history. They are to be found in everyday life. That is David's experience. And if we had time to look more thoroughly at Saul, we would see that Saul did not prove God in the little things. That's why, when faced now with the big thing, he's totally powerless.

You know the story. David said, 'If no one else will go, I'll go.' And he took five stones and a sling, and Goliath thought it was a joke (verses 41–44): sticks and stones are what you bring to drive dogs away.

But I love what David said to him (verses 45–47): 'You come against me with sword and spear and javelin, but I come against you in the name of the Lord Almighty, the God of the armies of Israel, whom you have defied. . . . All those gathered here will know that it is not by sword or spear that the Lord saves; for the battle is the Lord's, and he will give all of you into our hands.'

That doesn't mean David didn't have to take aim. He did. But as he did so, he said, 'Goliath, God has made a promise; therefore, God will not revoke that promise. You are going to die.' And with that confidence in God's ability, he slung the stone. Goliath fell to the ground, David went up, took Goliath's sword from his sheaf and cut off his head.

At last, in Saul's experience, the Philistines have been defeated. But not because of Saul; rather, because of a man—indeed, a boy—who was prepared to let God be God, to take God at His word, believe it, take the risk, and step out with the confidence that God was going to intervene.

And this, I tell you, is a principle of Christian living, not just Christian service. God calls you to be holy. Everything in the world will stop you being holy. You say, 'Lord Jesus, You called me; You who called me are faithful; You do it, as I obey You and trust You.'

But just one last thing. I want to say to you this morning, you're one of two people here; you're either a Saul or a David.

By a Saul, I mean you're called by God, you have experience of God. Saul is not a pagan; he's a God-ordained, God-experienced man. He speaks the language of godliness. When David went to fight, Saul said to him, 'Go, and the Lord be with you' (17:37).

Let me tell you something, that was meaningless language to Saul. He did not believe God would be with David. If he had, he would have believed God would have been with himself. He would have gone forty days before. So here's a man who's learnt the language; and it's easier to learn the language than to learn the life. There are people who speak the language who know little of the life. Saul was like that.

Or are you a David? That is, a man or woman prepared to take risks, to step out in the confidence that God is bigger than every situation, and that if He has declared His will on the matter, there's no further discussion necessary. You believe God, and then you act in the confidence He is going to intervene.

There is more I would have said about David, but our time is gone. You'll have to find out for yourself what happened to him. If you think Saul congratulated David, you don't understand human nature. Do you think Saul patted him on the back and said, 'Great stuff, David, thank you for letting us off the hook'? No. Saul became his enemy—angry, jealous, attempting to kill him. David was a fugitive for the rest of Saul's life.

On Monday morning I finished with a question: Is it ritual or reality? On Tuesday morning, I asked: Is it Ichabod or Ebenezer? This morning I want to ask you a question again: Are you Saul or David? Called by God—I am not questioning your Christian life or calling. But are you like Saul—'It's all dead language now'? Or are you like David—'God is real—real! And we trust Him.'

4. Selective Obedience
(1 Samuel 13–15)

It has been a wonderful privilege to open the Scriptures in these morning Bible Readings, and what has been so encouraging has been the appetite that there's been here for the word of God, and through that the appetite for the Lord Jesus and for God Himself. It's been a great joy for me, and I trust that God has spoken.

I hope that many of us will realise that we're not called to be New Testament Christians but Bible Christians. We impoverish ourselves if we limit our Christianity to the New Testament. There's far more Old Testament than New. It's the only Bible Jesus preached from, the only Bible the apostles preached from, and it was enough to make Timothy wise unto salvation, and there are so many truths in it. I would encourage you to dig deep into the Old Testament and not be frightened by some things that are not easy.

And we do have to think hard; some parts of the Old Testament, I think, were not intended for reading so much as for studying. Books like Leviticus; you try reading them, they get a little bit tedious, but you study them and they're rich. In fact, there are more of the words of God spoken in the first person in the book of Leviticus than any other book in the Bible. Some of you may have a red-letter edition of the Bible—all the words of Jesus are in red. If somebody was to devise, let's say, a green-letter edition, where all the words of God were in green, Leviticus would be a very green book. But it's probably one of the least read books in your Bible. Yet we should study books like that, dig under their surface, not just reading isolated verses but seeking the heartbeat of what is being said in the writing and compiling of them.

Of course there are lots of details and events in 1 Samuel that we've had to pass by. I've had to be selective and, rather than try to cover so much that in fact one says very little, I've tried to major in on what seems to me to be the heart of the message of the book. If I were to give a title to these four studies, I would call them 'Maintaining Spiritual Reality'.

We have seen in each session the contrast between reality and unreality. This morning, I want us to look in chapters 13—15 of 1 Samuel. And if we took a broader run through Saul's life yesterday, this morning we're going to narrow it down to these three chapters.

Let me just remind you of what we saw yesterday. Saul had a history of God's involvement in his life. God had chosen him, you remember. He had changed Saul's heart. The Holy Spirit had come upon him in power (chapter 10). And yet, in the one area where God had been specific about his reign—his deliverance of Israel from the Philistines—he experienced only forty years of disaster. And we looked at the three records of battle with the Philistines, culminating in the death of Saul fighting them on Mount Gilboa.

This morning we're going to look at something that is perhaps even more important than that in Saul's life. Not only did he lose his battle with the Philistines, but he lost the kingship, the kingdom, the right to rule. The God who had given him the throne took him off the throne. He was disqualified, and God said, in the very strong words of chapter 16 that we'll be looking at later, 'I have rejected Saul from being king over Israel.'

And it was Samuel, who had first recognised and announced Saul's kingship, who was called upon to pronounce God's judgement on him and the taking of the kingdom from him.

This happened twice, in two different circumstances, but for one underlying reason. And we look this morning at these two circumstances; firstly, and more briefly, at chapter 13; and secondly—and we'll devote most of our time to it and its implications—the second incident in chapter 15.

Saul is in battle with the Philistines at Geba (13:8). We looked at that in some detail yesterday. You remember, when Saul gathered with three thousand men against the huge Philistine army. The response of Saul and his men was to quake with fear (verse 7).

The story continues in verses 8–14. Saul is expecting Samuel to arrive within seven days; that is clear, because he waited for him. But Samuel did not come. So Saul took into his own hands a priestly function, offering the burnt offering and the fellowship offering before God. It was a responsibility that belonged exclusively to the priesthood, and Samuel, in addition to being a judge and a prophet, was also a priest. He was also a very busy man.

You can read in 1 Chronicles 6 that he was a descendant of Levi through Kohath. He took on the priesthood. You recall, he grew up in Shiloh and received the training there from Eli, and now he was exercising the priestly function as well.

The priest alone, the Levitical priest, had the right to offer the burnt offering before God. And because Samuel had not arrived, Saul, knowing that the Philistines were about to beat them and afraid to go and fight them as he should have done, thought, 'Well, at least I can appeal to God, and maybe God will intervene.' Under the pressure of the circumstances, he exercised his own judgement over the revealed will of God. He explained to Samuel later (verse 11): 'When I saw that the men were scattering, and that you did not come at the set time, and that the Philistines were assembling at Michmash, I thought, "Now the Philistines will come down against me at Gilgal, and I have not sought the Lord's favour." So I felt compelled to offer the burnt offering.'

Compelled by what? Compelled by the pressure of circumstances to disobey what God had revealed as His will. Have you ever found yourself in that kind of situation, where circumstances are such that, although you know the will of God in some area you feel, 'In this instance, I will exercise my own judgement, and do what I think is right; because although God makes general rules, this is an exception'?

I tell you, I've sat and counselled with people—even this week at Keswick—who, in a particular circumstance, have felt that though God has revealed a general will for us, 'in my particular case things are different'.

So Saul offered the burnt offering to God, and as a result of that Samuel told him, 'You acted foolishly' (verse 13). And later; 'If you had [obeyed God's command], God would have established your kingdom over Israel for all time. But now your kingdom will not endure.'

To Saul, what he did was reasonable. To his men who were with him, it was a sensible act in the circumstances; they were beginning to scatter. But to God it was sin. It was disobedience. And there are not various degrees of disobedience. To do what is right in your own eyes, if it conflicts with the revealed will of God, is sin.

Now turn to chapter 15, and another circumstance altogether. But there's the same underlying failure in Saul's heart. And this is the second incident that precipitates Samuel's statement that Saul would lose the throne and the kingdom.

The instructions recorded in verses 1–3 are very clear. The Hebrew verb translated 'totally destroy' is repeated seven times in this chapter. God made no bones about His instructions. There's no ambiguity. They seem to us, of course, to be particularly barbaric instructions, especially when He declares that he is to destroy men, women, children and infants, and all the cattle, sheep, camels and donkeys. But we need to understand the reason for this, and it comes in verse 2: 'I will punish the Amalekites for what they did to Israel when they waylaid them as they came up from Egypt.'

Let me take a moment to explain that and who these Amalekites are, and why they're under the wrath of God to this extent. Amalek was a grandson of Esau. You find his birth in Genesis 36. You remember that Esau was the older of the twins, and Esau and his descendants (generally known as the Edomites) are set in Scripture in contrast with Jacob and his descendants, the Israelites. Jacob represents the elect of God, and Esau and the Edomites represent the non-elect.

You may remember that statement in Malachi chapter 1, 'Jacob have I loved but Esau have I hated', quoted by Paul in Romans chapter 9. We're not going to talk about the meaning of election now (though I have very strong convictions that it's a largely misunderstood doctrine) except in this context, to establish an important principle behind this instruction given through Samuel.

The Amalekites—as part of the family of Esau whose grandson gave his name to this tribe, and as related therefore to the Edomites—are representative of all that is outside the purposes of God, of the non-elect. More than that, they are depicted in Scripture as being the enemies of God.

Verse 2 refers back to the time Israel left Egypt. It was the Amalekites who waylaid them; the first enemy they encountered after leaving Egypt. That incident, recorded in Exodus 17:8, is necessary to an adequate understanding of the instruction in 1 Samuel 15. You remember the story, of course. Joshua led the army into the battle down in the valley; Moses went to the top of the hill, and held his staff in the air; and, as he tired, Aaron and Hur, either side of him, helped him.

And this, of course, teaches an important principle; that victory over the enemies of God is not won but received. It's appropriated by faith. It was not Joshua in the valley who won the victory, it was Moses on the hill who won it. It's the same with victory in your life and mine; that's one of the great truths of the New Testament.

Joshua didn't win the battle, God gave the victory. And they won it, they overcame the Amalekites. But that wasn't the end—verse 14: 'Then the Lord said to Moses [now listen to this], "Write this on a scroll as something to be remembered and make sure that Joshua hears it, because I will completely [blot out] the memory of [Amalek] from under heaven." '

That's God's declared intention.

Turn now to Deuteronomy 25:17–19, where we find something else about the Amalekites. We need to understand this, and then we will see its relevance, and the principles that are relevant to you and me this morning. God says here: 'Remember what the Amalekites did to you along the way when you came out of Egypt. When you were weary and worn out, they met you on your journey [which is typical of the enemies of God] and cut off all who were lagging behind; they had no fear of God.

When the Lord your God gives you rest from all the enemies around you in the land he is giving you to possess as an inheritance, you shall blot out the memory of Amalek from under heaven. Do not forget!' God begins and ends that statement with a warning to remember what the Amalekites did.

'This is My will,' says God, 'to wipe out the Amalekites.' They stand as the enemies of God and of the people of God; the enemies of all that God would do, intent on diverting and preventing and obstructing His purposes. That's the principle.

Turn back now to 1 Samuel 15:4, because here is the opportunity for Saul to fulfil that declared will of God, and He has given him the instructions. In obedience, he summons his men. He even warns the Kenites to get out of the way; 'Don't be anywhere near the scene of battle, we're going to destroy these Amalekites. Get out of the way, so that you don't get involved in it.'

His intentions begin well; and he does destroy them— but with one or two good exceptions. In verse 8, he kept Agag, the king of the Amalekites, alive. That probably seemed a strategic move to Saul. 'He can provide us with intelligence, with information. We can use this man alive better than dead.'

They took the best, it says—the best of the sheep and the cattle, the calves, the lambs. Everything that was good. Why destroy good sheep, good calves, good cows? Let's be selective. We'll keep what's good. And he exercised his own judgement in what was good.

When Samuel arrives, Saul meets him and says, 'I've carried out the Lord's instructions; I've done what God has said; we've gained victory over the Amalekites.' Samuel replies, 'What, then, is the bleating of the sheep that God told you to destroy? What is the lowing of the cattle that God demanded should be slain?' Samuel is saying, in effect, 'There are the sounds of life here, where God has sentenced death.'

May I make this personal just for a moment? Because the only value of studying the Scriptures is not that we should be steeped in more Bible information, but that we might know the penetration of its effect into our own hearts. I want to ask you—and I'm going to come back to this later—is there something in your life this morning that God has sentenced to death? God has declared His will about that thing; it has no place in your life if you're going to be a believer and walk humbly with God—but you've kept it.

Just as with Saul, it's something good; it's the best of what God had condemned; the best of the sheep and the cattle. Is there some sin in somebody's life here this morning, and you know that, as the revealed will of God, this should have no place, but you've been able to rationalise it—that there's a way in which this particular thing can be used for good?

Are you playing with fire in a relationship that you know is not the will of God, but which you have convinced yourself can be used in some good way? Is there some ambition that you hold that you know God has condemned? Is there some habit that you've learned to tolerate over the years; you've ceased to declare war on it because you've learned to live with it? As with Saul, it may be something that you consider good, but God has said it must go. I want to say this, that the best of what God has condemned is condemned. Even the best.

If you read through the book of Judges you find a continuous cycle of God raising up a judge and bringing victory, and then the people going back into their bondage and sin and usually being overrun by some enemy. There's a recurring phrase in Judges: 'Each man did what was right in his own eyes.' Not 'they did what was wrong'. If you were willingly holding on to something that was wrong, and you agreed with God it was wrong, you probably wouldn't be at Keswick this week—unless you were some spiritual masochist—because you would know God would put His finger on it sooner or later. But perhaps there's something else, that is right in your eyes.

This is Saul's situation, you see. But the best of what God condemns remains condemned. And if we're going to go home from Keswick this week full of the Holy Spirit, equipped to live godly lives that have a cutting edge to them, then there's got to be a time when God puts His finger on that which He's condemned and that you've retained.

For a number of years now I have been an avid reader of the 'Keswick Week'. Ever since 1892 the Keswick addresses have been in some form written down and published. Some years ago I came across one of the old 'Keswick Weeks' in a second-hand bookshop; I bought it, read it and was thrilled by it, and I began to collect them. I've got about ninety-five of them now.

And twice in the history of Keswick there's been revival to some degree, where God has worked unusually. Once was in 1905, in the aftermath of the Welsh Revival; a whole contingent came from Wales. The other time was in 1922, when a man called Douglas Brown had been invited here to give the Bible Readings, though in fact he didn't. He said in his first address he wasn't going to and he didn't. So he never came back (I looked through later volumes to check). I wonder if anybody here was here in 1922? In 1921 there had been a revival in East Anglia, one of the unreported revivals in this country this century; it began in Lowestoft, and it happened under the ministry of this man Douglas Brown. In 1921 two afternoons were given over here at Keswick to report on that revival. In

1922 Douglas Brown came here to give his (supposedly!) Bible Readings, but he preached about revival.

On the Thursday morning of that week he preached on this verse in 1 Samuel 15: 'What then is the bleating of sheep in my ears? What is this lowing of cattle that I hear?' He called his address, The Tragic Bleating of a Defective Consecration. At the end of it, he challenged folks to deal with the bleating sheep in their lives, with the lowing cattle; the things God had condemned that they had retained. At the end of the meeting he invited people to go with him to the Drill Hall in Keswick. It held two hundred seats, and they couldn't get everybody in. So they came back into this hall. There were between two and three thousand people on this site, though not of course in this particular tent, on their knees crying out to God for forgiveness. Christians with bleating sheep; things God had condemned. And lowing cattle; things God had sentenced to death, and they had retained.

And I wonder this morning if there are not in your heart, as I speak, the bleating sheep and the lowing cattle of the Holy Spirit's voice: saying to you, 'If you want to know the victory and the power of God that was available to Saul, but which he was about to lose because of this incident with the Amalekites; if in your heart you want to go home from Keswick not just with a few more ideas and a bit more information and a memory of the good atmosphere, but to be a man or a woman who is going to be a channel for God to be released through you—then you've got to deal with those bleating sheep and lowing cattle.'

Some of you are going home to Christian ministry, the mission-field, the pastorate, evangelism, whatever it is to which God has called you; some of you to secular work, your home, perhaps to eldership, leadership in your church. Whatever it is—and I stress this without apology because it was a burden to me as I prayed about this session and asked God to help me select the right things to say—you've got to deal with the things Saul did not deal with. It cost Saul his throne. In verse 26, the judgement of God is pronounced.

And, of course, he justifies himself (verse 20): he blames the soldiers. But God isn't interested in the soldiers, he's interested in Saul. You can find a reason why somebody else has encouraged you to sin, I'm sure. That's true through history ever since the Garden of Eden.

He goes on to say an incredibly subtle and dangerous thing (verse 21): 'The soldiers took sheep and cattle from the plunder, the best of what was devoted to God, in order to sacrifice them to the Lord your God at Gilgal.'

'Samuel,' says Saul, 'you don't understand. We kept what was good, not for selfish reasons but in order to serve God in sacrifice with these sheep and cattle.'

Samuel makes that great statement, probably the best known verse in this chapter, one of the familiar verses of 1 Samuel, verse 22:

> But Samuel replied: 'Does the Lord delight in burnt offerings and sacrifices as much as in obedience to the voice of the Lord? To obey is better than to sacrifice, and to heed is better than the fat of rams. For rebellion is like the sin of divination, and arrogance like the evil of idolatry.'

'Listen,' says Samuel. 'You may have kept them for a good reason...'

There may be somebody here who believes that a particular wrong relationship is a means of God working in that person's life. You're playing with fire. God does not want your sacrifice that derives from sheep that shouldn't live. That's the implication here. It's your obedience that He wants; cold-blooded obedience, even when you don't see why God has declared this.

What does God look for when He looks at your heart and mine? It's not even our worship. If I understand Samuel's priorities, it's your obedience He wants. Out of your obedience will come worship that's true, in spirit and truth.

We're going to break the bread and share the wine of the Lord's Supper this evening. This is why we are told 'Let a man examine himself'. It's your obedience God is looking for. Out of that obedient heart your worship will be real. And the measure of our spiritual life is not our Christian service nor the record of God's blessing through our lives; it's our attitude, our disposition of obedience towards God.

Of course, we will all sin. 'If any man says he has no sin he deceives himself,' John tells us. He won't deceive his wife or his neighbours; he'll probably deceive himself. We're not talking about sinlessness, we're talking about a disposition and attitude of obedience, an attitude towards God. Yes, you'll fall!

I like to understand it in this way: when I got married, I made a commitment to my wife; 'Forsaking all others, I take you only unto me.' For the ten years that we've been married I have lived like that; never looked at another girl, never wanted or needed to. But stating that commitment didn't make me behave that way. It required a disposition.

I'm not asking you this morning, 'Is there no record of disobedience in your life?' That's not the point; there will be. I'm asking about your *disposition*. If you asked my wife, 'Has Charles been a perfect husband?', she wouldn't even wait for you to finish the question! But it's the disposition, it's the attitude of heart, that God looks for.

We've seen Saul's fundamental attitude, in chapters 13 and 15: 'I reserve the freedom to exercise my own judgement over what God has declared; when I can see a better way, when I can see a rational reason for my sin.' And, generally speaking, he says, 'I did obey; we did destroy everybody except Agag, and most of the sheep and cattle.' But that isn't the point. It's the fact that he left undone those things that he ought to have done.

Do you know why this is so important? I'll tell you. Turn to 2 Samuel chapter 1, where we have a second account of Saul's death, with a little more detail. From verse 1, for example, we learn that there were some Amalekites outside that particular group that Saul had encountered. Agag was only destroyed in chapter 15, but there were clearly others still within the brief that God gave Samuel, because Saul must totally destroy the Amalekites. Clearly there were some that he hadn't dealt with, and David here is fighting them.

On the third day (verse 2) the Amalekite arrives from Saul's camp. Now, you remember yesterday, that Saul was wounded. He asked his armour-bearer to finish him off; he refused to do so. So Saul, it says, fell on his own sword and died. Well, it's very clear from this chapter that when he fell, or leaned, on his sword, he missed the heart or whatever would have killed him quickly, and he was not quite dead. So in 2 Samuel 1:9 here he is, on his spear, not quite dead: and he appeals to the Amalekite. 'I tried to finish myself off, but I haven't done so. Would you please, Amalekite, finish me off?' So the Amalekite killed him, took his crown and arm-band, and brought them to David.

Saul, facing death at the hands of the Philistines, tried to commit suicide; he hadn't quite finished himself off; and who came along? It just happened to be an Amalekite, one of the group of men and women of whom God had said, 'Utterly destroy them', and Saul had failed to destroy. And the Amalekite happened to be around in a battle; nothing to do with the Amalekites. He just happened to be around to put the knife into Saul's back, and, I think significantly, to take the crown from his head. God called Saul; Samuel ordained him, but God put the crown on his head. It was an Amalekite who took it off.

There's a very frightening lesson there. The sin you fail to deal with when God tells you to, that thing He tells you to destroy; if you don't destroy it, it may come back one day and destroy you. You see, sin never hits you over-night.

I'm talking now about major sins; we know sometimes of Christians, sometimes leaders, who fall, and we're shocked. We gasp; we say, 'How did it happen?' But I tell you, long before that sin, whether it's adultery, embezzling money from the funds, whatever it may be—long before that act took place they refused to destroy its seeds in their heart, and they tolerated them and played with them, played around, took chances, tolerated what God condemned. And one day it grew all too powerful, and when they were weak, like Saul now on the battlefield, those sins were there to put the knife in and take the crown off the head.

Is that a frightening picture?

Contrast this with David, yesterday. You remember when he came to fight Goliath? He said to Saul, 'I have proved God in the lesser circumstances, I've proved Him in the little areas; now I'm prepared to trust Him in the big crises, and face Goliath.'

That's David. Saul is the complete opposite. It was in the little things, where he chose something that was good, not bad. And the seeds of that disobedience resulted in the Amalekite whom he preserved taking the crown off his head, having put the knife into his back.

Do you remember the story of Esther? When a man called Haman wanted to utterly destroy all the Jews in the Persian Empire? He was the Adolf Hitler of Persia. He wanted to destroy the Jewish race. Do you know who Haman was, in Esther chapter 3? He's introduced as Haman the son of Hammedatha the Agagite. Who was Agag? The king that Saul did not kill. He may have been a descendant; it may be that 'the Agagite' is a royal title; but he was an Amalekite.

Saul refused to obey God and utterly destroy them, and they not only came back to destroy Saul but threatened to destroy the whole Jewish race.

And in the New Testament, do you know whose ancestry can probably be traced back to the Amalekite? Herod, who killed all the baby children in Bethlehem in an attempt to wipe out the Messiah—Herod was an Edomian. You can trace his line back to the Edomites, relatives of the Amalekites.

You do not know when what you tolerate today as good will come back. But it will. I remember once reading a story of a circus act in which a man allowed a huge python to wrap itself around him until its coils completely covered him. The audience would watch in horror until he uttered the word of command, and the snake would unwind itself and slither away, and they would break into applause. But one night he gave the command and nothing happened, and as the audience watched, the python's coils pulled tighter and tighter until they heard bones crack and the man shrieking. Some of the circus staff realised what was happening, killed the python and dragged it off the man. But he was already crushed to death.

The man was renowned for his handling of snakes. He'd got the python when it was very small, taken it home and kept it and others with him. They'd slept in his bedroom, travelled in his pockets, ridden in his car. He was with them twenty-four hours a day. They probably thought he was just an unusually-shaped python. It was his training strategy. And he taught them tricks.

You see, when he first got the python it was so small he could have crushed it in his fingers, but he didn't. He said, 'I'll play with this; I'll train it, I'll keep it.' Until one day it crushed him.

Let me tell you, that's the story of Saul, who kept the best of what God condemned—'because I think it's good'—and it came back to destroy him. And as a consequence, Samuel pronounced judgement on him and left him.

'I will not go back with you. You have rejected the word of the Lord, and the Lord has rejected you as king over Israel!'
1 Samuel 15:26

Then Samuel left for Ramah, but Saul went up to his home in Gibeah of Saul. Until the day Samuel died, he did not go to see Saul again, though Samuel mourned for him. And the Lord was grieved that he had made Saul king over Israel.
   The Lord said to Samuel, 'How long will you mourn for Saul, since I have rejected him as king over Israel? Fill your horn with oil and be on your way; I am sending you to Jesse of Bethlehem. I have chosen one of his sons to be king.'
1 Samuel 15:34—16:1

Aren't those sad words? This is the God who had called Saul to the throne, now saying, 'I have rejected him.' But don't misunderstand that; Saul had rejected God. And God even says to Samuel, 'Don't even mourn for him.'

Sometimes—and this is what I learn from that—sometimes we can waste our time mourning for those who have gone off the rails by their own choice. They chose it.

Although God had called Saul to the throne and promised him all kinds of things, we must never, we *can* never presume on the promises of God. We walk humbly with God, in the fear of God. Because, if I turn my back even over something I think is good, God's hand will have gone from my life. Saul stayed on the throne for many more years, but God wasn't with him. The Spirit of God left him. That was of course an Old Testament thing; now we're sealed to the day of redemption. I'm not talking about salvation, I'm talking about service. The Spirit of God, in service, to which He's called you and commissioned you, can be withdrawn; but you chose it.

As I was praying about this Bible Reading, I began to feel very much the importance of realising that this is of practical value, not just of cerebral interest. I know God has spoken to many people this week—and there are some that He's spoken to again this morning, who have gone through these Bible Readings, and maybe looked into that word and seen in the mirror that it's not reality, it's ritual; it's not Ebenezer, 'God with us', it's Ichabod, 'the glory departed'. God has spoken, and it will be a tragedy to leave Keswick not having settled those issues about which He's spoken.

Let me recap very briefly. Two reasons why Saul lost the throne:

First, he did what he should not have done. He offered burnt offerings, which was the task solely of the priest.

Second, he did not do what he should have done, in destroying the Amalekites.

If God has spoken to us through this week, you and I need to respond to whatever it is God has spoken to us about. Some bleating of sheep that God has sentenced to death, still bleating in your heart; some lowing of cattle that he's condemned and you've called good. In a moment of silence, I want you to put that right with God. It may mean you've got to go home, or out of this tent, and put things right with other people too. Then I'm going to pray for you, for those who have made a response in their hearts. Let's have a moment of prayer. As God has spoken, respond to Him, and repent of that which needs repenting of silently in your own heart.

Mr Price concluded his final Bible Reading with an invitation to those intent upon putting things right with God, to stand, in testimony of their determination to do so, as he led the congregation in prayer.

THE ADDRESSES

THREE APPROACHES TO SIN

by Dr Warren Wiersbe

Proverbs 28:13

The most costly things in the world are salvation and sin. Salvation is costly to God because sin is so costly to man. And because sin is so costly it can rob us of that which is beautiful, blessed, wholesome and holy. The word of God reminds us repeatedly that God's children must deal deeply and decisively with sin.

It isn't my purpose tonight to put anyone under a guilt-trip. It's my purpose tonight to magnify the mercy and grace of God in the forgiveness of sin. But if I'm going to deal decisively and deeply with sin, the way Jesus told me to—by surgery—I must understand something about it. If my spiritual surgery is to be sincere and successful, it must be according to the word and the Spirit of God.

When it comes to dealing with sin in my life, there are only three possible approaches I can take. And these are summarised in the word of God:

> He who conceals his sins does not prosper, but whoever confesses and renounces them finds mercy.
>
> *Proverbs 28:13*

Nobody here gets up in the morning and says, 'I'm

going to make this a good day; I'm going to sin.' On the
contrary, we say, 'Our Father, Thy will be done; lead me
not into temptation.' Here then are three possible
approaches to dealing with sin in our lives, and it's something that we want to do.

We can conceal our sin

The first possible approach is, we can conceal our sin.
Now this is my natural response. When I was born with
Adam's nature I found myself leaning toward Adam's
methods of dealing with things.

You'll recall that when our first parents sinned they ran
away and hid; fear came in. And then when God con-
fronted them with what they had done, deception came in.
Adam blamed Eve, and Eve blamed the serpent. I suppose ultimately they were blaming God—'The woman
You gave me...the serpent that You made.'

So my first inclination is to conceal my sin, even though
the word of God tells me that those who did so did not
prosper. Cain did it. 'Am I my brother's keeper?' Achan
did it; God found him out. David did it; that tragic blot in
David's memory. 'When I kept silence,' he wrote—'when
I kept silence my bones waxed old within me.' And David,
who was so young and virile, so full of life and song—put
down his sword, pick up his harp—was walking around
like an old man. The springs of life within him had dried
up because he covered his sin.

Ananias and Sapphira did it. They sold a piece of
property, kept part of the price. They could have kept all
the price. Campbell Morgan said that the sin of Ananias
and Sapphira was not in stealing money from God; it was
trying to make people think they were more spiritual than
they really were. Some of us perhaps have tried that.

Our natural response is to conceal our sin. How do we
do it? I'd like to invite you to turn to 1 John 1:5. Three

times in that passage John says 'If we claim'. Notice the sequence: verse 6, verse 8, verse 10. Here is concealing sin by what we claim. We're lying, we're deceiving.

In verse 6, we're lying to each other. The word for this in the Bible is hypocrisy. People sometimes come to us and say, 'I feel such an awful hypocrite.' And I say, 'Why?' 'Well, I'm just not living up to what I know.' But who does?

Hypocrisy is not missing the mark when you're striving; hypocrisy is trying to make people think you've hit the target and you aren't even shooting. The word means an actor, one who wears a mask. How do we conceal our sin? By deceiving one another.

But it gets worse. 'He who conceals his sins does not prosper.' It doesn't say he *will* not prosper. When he starts concealing sin, something starts to happen down inside.

One of God's purposes in salvation is the building of character. We talk about getting God's work done; the first thing God does is build the worker. And God's more concerned about the worker than He is about the work. That's why He spent so much time with Jonah.

Jonah preached at the greatest evangelistic meeting in Bible history and hated the people he was preaching to. We would have ended the book at chapter 3. The city got saved; what else matters? Jonah matters. So God continues in chapter 4, dealing with His servant. Why? He wants to build character. He had an angry preacher on His hands.

What begins in verse 6 with lying to others gets worse in verse 8: 'If we claim to be without sin, we deceive ourselves and the truth is not in us.' Now we're lying to ourselves. That's not hypocrisy, it's duplicity. It's possible for a child of God to try to deceive himself. 'I've had my devotions.' Ah, but they didn't touch my heart; I'm going back to the same old life. 'Oh, but I've been to a service.' Ah, but it didn't change me.

Then in verse 10 it gets worse. Now I'm lying to God and making God a liar: 'If we claim we have not sinned, we make him out to be a liar and his word has no place in our lives.' When we start living by lies, there's no room for truth.

You notice the sequence. In verse 6, we're not living by the truth; in verse 8, the truth is not in us; in verse 10, the word has no place in us. And yet it's possible for me to go through the external activities of a Christian walk and be concealing sin. It's frightening.

In the first two chapters of 1 John, the apostle deals with fellowship. His illustration is of light versus darkness. In chapters 3, 4 and 5, he deals with sonship, and it's a matter not of light and darkness but life and death. The key phrase in chapters 3, 4 and 5 is 'born of God', 'born of God', 'born of God'. But in 1 and 2, we're walking with God. He's talking about fellowship. And he's saying we're either walking in the light, which means living by truth, or we're walking in the darkness.

When you hit upon a spiritual truth, some fundamental principle that just thrills your heart, do you ever go through the Bible looking for illustrations of it? I recommend that to you. I was pondering John's discussion of light and darkness, and I said, 'Now, where do we find in the Bible people who started in the light but ended in the darkness?' Well, there are several.

King Saul. Early in the morning as the sun was coming up, says 1 Samuel 9, Samuel took Saul off by himself, anointed him, kissed him and made him king over Israel. His life began in the dawning of a new day. How did it end? At night, disguised, going to a witch's lair, seeking for help, and then ultimately dying on the battlefield after trying to commit suicide.

Samson. The very name 'Samson' means 'sunny'. He brightened up the home when he came. God endued this young man with power, and then he began to go downhill. And where did he end up? Blinded, in the darkness. I know at the end of his life he brought down the house, and he killed more in his death than he did during his life—I know all of that; but I am also reminding myself of the fact that he started in the light and he ended in the darkness. Why?

Saul lied to other people. 'I have done the will of the Lord,' he said to Samuel. 'We kept the best of the spoils to sacrifice to the Lord.' Doesn't that sound pious!

Saul lied to others; Samson lied to himself. He'd sin and say, 'Well, I got away with that.' And when that ultimate night came, he woke up and said, 'I'm going to shake myself like I always do.' But his power was gone.

Judas. Judas walked with the light for probably three years, and as the treasurer of the disciples' group was an intimate of the Lord Jesus. I think one of the most ominous statements in the Gospel of John, which is a Gospel of symbolism, is 'And Judas went out and it was night.' And for Judas it still is night, and it always will be night.

Saul lied to others; Samson lied to himself; Judas tried to lie to God; and all three ended up in the dark.

'He who conceals his sins does not prosper.' Psalm 51 makes that very clear. 'Oh,' you say, 'we've read that so often.' Would you look at it again?

David committed two great sins in his life; a sin of the flesh, Bathsheba, and a sin of the spirit, numbering the people. From the sin of Bathsheba four people died, from the sin of numbering the people seventy thousand people died. He married Bathsheba. God gave them a son whom David loved dearly—Solomon.

When he numbered the people, he bought a piece of property, erected an altar there and offered a sacrifice to

God: 'Oh Lord, touch me; don't touch these sheep.' And God heard his prayer and stopped the plague.

The interesting thing is that one day Solomon, who was born of Bathsheba, took that piece of property that was purchased because of David's sin, and built a temple on it. Only God can take a man's two greatest sins and build a temple out of it. Where sin abounds grace much more abounds.

That's not an excuse for sin; David paid dearly. But I'll tell you what it is: it's an encouragement for when the devil accuses you!

What did it cost David?

Verse 3: something happened to his eyes. 'My sin is always before me.' Verse 6: something happened to his mind. 'Teach me wisdom in the inmost place.' Verse 8: something happened to his ears, 'Let me hear joy and gladness', and something happened to his bones: 'Let the bones you have crushed rejoice.'

Something happened to his heart, verse 10: 'Create in me a pure heart, O God, and renew a steadfast spirit within me.' Verse 11: something happened to his power. 'Do not cast me from your presence or take your Holy Spirit from me' (as God did with Saul). Verse 12: something happened to his joy. 'Restore to me the joy of your salvation.'

Something happened to his mouth—David was always ready with a song, a witness or a prayer, but his mouth had been closed: 'Then I will teach transgressors your ways.' Verse 14: 'My tongue will sing of your righteousness. O Lord, open my lips, and my mouth will declare your praise.'

We can conceal our sins, but if we do, we won't prosper. There is that deterioration on the inside and that discipline on the outside, and we're miserable.

Well, thank God, our verse doesn't end there:

He who conceals his sins does not prosper, but whoever confesses and renounces them finds mercy.

We can conceal our sin, or,

We can confess our sin

Now, that takes us back once again to 1 John chapter 1, a verse that some people use as an evangelical good-luck charm, saying, 'I will go out and sin because I know I can come back and confess it.'

But that's not what John is saying. 'If we confess our sins, he is faithful and just and will forgive us our sins and purify us from all unrighteousness' (verse 9).

Now, what is he saying here? The word 'confess' means 'to say the same thing'. If I say the same thing about what I have done as God's word says about it, then I can claim God's forgiveness.

That was the difference between David and Saul; Saul was good at excuses. I've noticed that people who are good at excuses are rarely good at anything else. Whenever Saul did something wrong he had an excuse; he could find somebody to blame.

That tragic request that he made to Samuel—'Honour me, please, before the people'—Saul's problem was pride. Samson's problem was lust; Judas's problem was covetousness. By the way, those are the three great sins that will wreck any ministry and put you in the dark.

'If we confess'—if we say the same thing as God says—that means I must go by God's definitions. It doesn't say, 'If we come with explanations.' He knows better than you or me why you did it. No, we don't come with explanations and we don't come with excuses. We come with confession; we come saying, 'Lord, according to Your word, my anger was murder, and I confess my sin. Lord, according to Your word, what I did was deception, and I come and confess my sin. I want to say the same thing about it You're saying.'

That's what David meant when he said, 'That you might be clear when you speak and true when you judge.' The difference between Saul and David was that David kept the word before him; Saul kept himself before him.

John is pleading for honesty; with God, with ourselves. 'I have to live with myself and so I want to be good for myself to know,' Edgar Guest wrote many years ago. It's true. You don't have to live with me (and there are probably some silent Amens going up at this point!) but you do have to live with yourself; I have to live with myself. I don't want to live with two selves, in duplicity.

Honest with God; honest with myself; and, where necessary in the sphere of confession, honest with one another. It doesn't mean we hang all of our dirty washing out in public. Unfortunately there are some evangelical exhibitionists who think that everybody wants to know what they've done. That's not always necessary. In fact, it can do damage. But in the sphere of influence, honest with one another.

'If we confess *our* sins'; it's personal. David said that God would not despise a broken and contrite heart. That encourages me, that God will not despise us when we come doing what Ezekiel said the Jews would do—loathing ourselves because of our sin. Not weeping because I got caught, nor because I'm hurt, nor because I'm being spanked; no. Anybody can do that. But coming and saying, 'I have sinned. How could I, a child of God, sin against such love? How could I, a student of God's word, sin against such light? How could I, one indwelt by the Holy Spirit, sin against the Holy Spirit?'—loathing ourselves.

Sin must be not only confessed, but judged, despised, and renounced.

Now, the promise is, if we confess our sins, He's faithful to His word and just toward His Son. Because Jesus died for our sins, and He was buried and He arose again, and today He is at the right hand of the Majesty on high, and He is our Advocate.

When I have problems with the law, I don't want a law book, I want a lawyer; when I'm sick, I don't want a medical book, I want a doctor; and when I've sinned, I need an Advocate in heaven. As my High Priest, He wants to give me grace to keep me from sinning, but if I sin, as my Advocate He waits for my confession of sin and then He forgives.

The picture of this is beautifully given in Zechariah chapter 3.

> Then he showed me Joshua the high priest standing before the angel of the Lord, and Satan standing at his right side to accuse him.
>
> *3:1*

It's a law court scene. Joshua, representing the nation, is dressed in filthy garments. Satan is standing there as the prosecuting attorney, accusing. When Satan talks to me about God, he lies, but often when he talks to God about me he tells the truth.

> The Lord said to Satan, 'The Lord rebuke you, Satan! The Lord, who has chosen Jerusalem, rebuke you! Is not this man a burning stick snatched from the fire?
>
> Now Joshua was dressed in filthy clothes as he stood before the angel. The angel said to those who were standing before him, 'Take off his filthy clothes.'
>
> Then he said to Joshua, 'See, I have taken away your sin, and I will put rich garments on you.'
>
> *3:2–4*

Sounds like the parable of the prodigal son! And the prophet got so enthusiastic...

> Then I said, 'Put a clean turban on his head.' So they put a clean turban on his head and clothed him, while the angel of the Lord stood by.
>
> *3:5*

When I have sinned Satan accuses. When I come to my heavenly Advocate who intercedes for me and represents me, it's not as though the Father is waiting to beat me and the Son has to say, 'No, don't do that.' No! The Father and the Son and the Holy Spirit work in perfect harmony and love. Satan accuses and says, 'Look what Wiersbe has done,' and then my Saviour steps up, bearing the wounds of Calvary—He took back to heaven the wicked works of men on His body—and He says, 'I died for him.'

The Lord rebukes Satan, the Lord removes the dirty clothing, the Lord restores Joshua with clean clothing, and that turban that had on the front of it a golden plate that read 'Holy to the Lord'.

We can conceal our sin, but if we do we won't prosper. We can confess our sin, and if we do He's faithful to His word and just toward His Son to forgive us and cleanse us.

But let's not stop there. There is a third approach we can take in dealing with our sins. He who conceals his sins does not prosper, but if we confess and renounce—forsake—our sins, we shall find mercy. That's what I need—mercy, mercy.

> Depth of mercy, can there be
> Mercy still reserved for me?

We can conquer our sin

Yes; yes. Because 1 John chapter 1 has another 'if'; 'If we claim'—that's concealing our sin; 'If we confess'—that's confessing our sin; but verse 7 says, 'If we walk'—that's conquering our sin.

It's not enough just to be forgiven, restored, reinstated, and then tumble again. No! We must conquer our sin. How? By walking in the light: 'If we walk in the light, as he is in the light'; 'as he is, so are we in this world'; 'as he is in the light'; 'we have fellowship with one another, and the blood of Jesus, his Son'—the work of Calvary—'purifies us from all sin'.

In the light of what? His word. 'Your word is a lamp to my feet, a light to my path...'; 'Your word have I hid in my heart that I may not sin against you...'; 'Now you are clean through the word...' How can a Christian keep clean in a dirty world and conquer sin if he ignores the word? Walking in the light of the word; walking in the light of the Lord in worship.

The greatest definition of worship in the English language, I think—and I've not read them all—is the one by Archbishop William Temple: 'For to worship God is to quicken the conscience with the holiness of God, feed the mind with the truth of God, purge the conscience with the beauty of God, open the heart to the love of God, devote the will to the service of God.'

That's walking in the light. God's church is a light; we're lampstands in a dark world. I don't think it's possible for a believer to conquer sin in isolation. We need each other. We need the fellowship of God's people if we're going to walk in the light. And as we walk in the light, so we can see the dirt coming; as we walk in the light, we have a better view of the path. As we walk in the light, particularly in the fellowship of God's people, there are those praying for us and standing with us, and the path becomes easier.

It's not enough just to confess sin. He said, 'Let's go on and conquer sin; let's put it away; let's forsake it, let's renounce it, by the power of the Holy Spirit of God.'

The most expensive things in the world are sin and salvation, and we have a God who pardons.

Again, I don't want anyone to be on a guilt-trip under a dark cloud. I'm not here to preach judgement, I'm here to preach mercy, and therefore I want to end with these marvellous words from the last chapter of Micah.

Let me read them to you. Remember our text, 'He who conceals his sins does not prosper but whoever confesses and renounces them shall find mercy.' The prophet says:

> Who is a God like you, who pardons sin and forgives the transgression of the remnant of his inheritance? You do not stay angry for ever but delight to show mercy. You will again have compassion on us; you will tread our sins underfoot and hurl all our iniquities into the depths of the sea.

God is waiting for me to turn my sin over to Him. He will hurl it into the depths of the sea, and it will be remembered no more. It will be as far as the east is from the west.

What shall we do with our sins? Cover them? No! Let's confess them and conquer them, by the grace of God!

THE MAKING OF A MAN OF GOD

by Rev. Ian Barclay

Ephesians 2:1–10

We're going to look at the opening verses of Paul's second chapter to the Ephesians, moving towards the possessions that we have in Jesus Christ. The chapter is about God establishing His people. You could say it really begins a long way before that; that it begins with God putting His hands down into the muck and mire of the human race, and with what He has in His hands, creating a people for Himself.

The marred material of the human race

The state of man's life without Christ
In the first three verses we find the marred material of the human race, the state of human life without Christ. 'As for you, you were dead in your transgressions and sins.'

There's something very final about that. Sin is not a deviation or sickness, something that means that we're a little off-balance in the way that we live. Sin is deadness, and that's very final.

It's comparatively easy to speak about that in a convention like the Keswick Convention. It becomes problematic when we go home to our family, to our neighbours, to our friends. We know some of them are outside Christ, but it's very difficult to look at them and say, 'Well, they're dead.'

Warren Wiersbe, in his book on Ephesians *Be Rich*, has a marvellous illustration of deadness. He points out that when our Lord Jesus Christ was on earth, so far as we know there were three people that He brought back to life; and they're very different.

Do you remember the first one, Jairus's daughter? When Jesus approached the scene, it was as though she was just asleep; warm, attractive, childlike; you would feel if you reached out your hand you could touch her and she would wake up. But she was dead. Some people are like that outside Christ; they're warm and they're attractive; but if they don't belong to Christ they're dead.

Do you remember the second person—the son of the widow of Nain? When Jesus approaches that scene the funeral is taking place, and if you could have looked into the coffin, you would have seen a corpse. Some people are like that outside Christ. They're corpse-like; it's easy to recognise that they're dead.

Remember the third person, Lazarus? Do you remember when Jesus approached that scene? The funeral had already taken place, he had been in the ground for a couple of days, and when Jesus started talking about bringing him back to life, they said, 'You can't do that.' The old translation has it marvellously; 'Behold he stinketh.' They don't have translations like that today.

Some people are like that outside Christ; we read about them day after day in our newspapers; they're so morally corrupt that they stink. The marred material of the human race; the state of human life outside Christ.

The sphere of man's activity outside Christ
I love the Revised Standard Version of Ephesians 2:2–3, with its repetition of the word 'following': 'following the

course of this world', 'following the prince of the power of
the air', 'following the desires of the body and mind'.

Following the course of this world. We know so many
people like that. Their aims, their ambitions, their aspira-
tions are all what they see on television or read about in
their Sunday colour supplements.

Following the prince of the power of the air. What's
your favourite name for him? My favourite name is
Beelzebub. They've just made a new film of William
Golding's book *Lord of the Flies*; the title is of course one
possible translation of 'Beelzebub'. I don't think it's the
best; I don't think it's the most biblical. I believe that the
best way to translate 'Beelzebub' is 'The lord of filth',
because that's where the flies come from.

You see, when the evil one Beelzebub comes to you
and says, 'Yes, of course, you can carry on worshipping in
that church, that fellowship; you can still go to the Keswick Convention—if you only bow your knee to me',
what he gives us is a Hollywood glossy image of himself.
But that soon disintegrates, and we see him as the lord of
filth. That's where he comes from.

Following the desires of the body and mind. This pres-
ents us with some problems, because most of the desires
that we have and the way that God gave them to us are
good things. We need to have the desire for food, or we
won't fuel this portable piece of plumbing that we carry
around with us every day. We need the desire for rest
because if we didn't rest this piece of plumbing, it would
cease functioning. We need the desire for sex because if
we didn't have that within our marriages the human race
would not continue.

But Paul's not talking about these being used in their
right way but their wrong way, where men and women
become *their* slaves and servants instead of these things
being *our* servants.

We live on the south coast, and a little while ago they had a Jaguar car owners' rally along the road where we live. I saw the car that I'd love to own if I only had that sort of money—the old SS100, with its enormous headlights, long bonnet, and open cockpit.

Now, imagine that your rich uncle has left you one of those, and you bring it to Keswick to show to everybody, and after the morning Bible Reading you say to somebody, 'Would you like to come out for a spin in my Jaguar?' And they say, 'Oh yes.' So you say, 'Hop in,' and you lean inside and let the handbrake off, and you make sure it's not in gear; and then you get behind the car and start pushing. And you push it round Windermere and Derwent Water. Later in the afternoon you're quite exhausted as you push it back.

And when you arrive back they say, 'Well, it's a remarkable car—but aren't cars meant to transport *you*? Do you have to do all that work?'

That's the sort of picture that Paul has in mind here, where men and women are being ruled by the desires of their body and mind. Would you underline that word 'mind'? I don't have any problem in recognising lust, sloth or gluttony. Yet God's people today are open to the most absurd suggestions that are being put into their minds, and they don't recognise it.

The sentence on man's nature outside Christ
Verse 3: 'We were by nature objects of wrath.'

Does that present you with problems? God's wrath is quite unlike man's anger; God never loses His temper, He's not subject to moods, He's never spiteful, He's never malicious, He doesn't take revenge.

Imagine that we decide to have a half-night of prayer for the United Kingdom, to start at 3 o'clock tomorrow morning. The first person to arrive makes sure that the lights are put on. Now, of course, when the lights are put on the darkness has to go. Light and darkness are mutually exclusive. They can't live with each other.

That's true of the holiness of God and the sinfulness of man. God's holiness and man's sinfulness mutually repel each other. They're exclusive. You see, if God wants to live with sinners He has to do one of two things; either He has to change Himself, which He cannot do because He is immutable, or He has to change us, which is what the gospel is all about; so that we can go to be with Him for ever.

'Ian Barclay, we're surprised at Keswick that you've taken a few minutes in quite a full programme to spell that out to us. We knew all that before we came to Keswick!'

Well, I've said it for three reasons:

Firstly, it's very likely that someone in this tent tonight has not found Christ. You need to find Him; you need to be born again.

Secondly, if we don't understand that outside Christ we're dead in our transgressions and sins, we'll never evangelise. We'll always imagine that our neighbours or our family or our friends will drift into the kingdom of God—but nobody has ever done that, because they're dead in their transgressions and sins; they need to hear the gospel of Jesus Christ—even if they're nice people.

And thirdly, I've said it because unless you understand this, you've got a wrong understanding of the church.

You see, when God decided to make His church, to take a people for Himself, He didn't take a few Scots and a few Englishmen and a few Welshmen and a few Irishmen and one or two people from Nebraska and say, 'Well, that'll be My kingdom.' No; He put His hand down into the muck and mire of the human race, and from what He has in His hands He created a church. He didn't choose gifted people; He chose the muck and the mire, and having got that muck and mire in His hands He forms His

church and He gifts His people as He will, for the work of
the ministry.

Do you sometimes say, 'I could never preach like they
do at Keswick!'? Please, don't ever say that. I was thrown
out of school as ineducable at the age of fifteen. My
headmaster told my parents that I'd probably end up a
criminal and I'd better be taken away. I went to work in
the city of London as a trader on the futures exchange—
you could do that in those days if you didn't have much
education and just wore the right sort of school tie—and
it was there that I heard about Christ. If Christ opened my
mind and changed my life, then He can do it for anyone.

Martin Luther said that Jesus Christ can carve rotten
wood and ride a lame horse. Remember how Paul put it in
1 Corinthians: God chose what is foolish and God chose
what is weak; God chose what is low and despised, and
even the things that are not, so that no human spirit might
boast in the presence of God.

The beautiful building of the community of God

Now look in verses 4–10 at the beautiful building that God
makes.

God starts His community
It starts with a marvellous 'But God'. You almost want to
ask, 'Well, but why?' And so Paul tells us why, and there
are four words that he uses, two in verse 4, and two in
verse 7.

The first word in verse 4 is 'mercy' (not first in the NIV
but as Paul actually wrote it). That's where it all begins:
God's mercy. The second word, again in verse 4, is 'love'.
That is the outreaching of the mercy of God. The third,
the first one in verse 7, is 'grace': 'The exceeding riches of
his grace'. And then again in verse 7 you've got that word
'kindness'. If grace bestows on me what I don't deserve,

the kindness of God adds richly to that. A beautiful building of the community of God.

God starts His community. Why, why did He choose us? Because of His mercy, because of His love, because of His grace, because of His kindness.

God shapes His community
I don't need to really say much about verse 5: 'By grace you have been saved.'

Everything that we're saying tonight is really encapsulated in that word 'saved'. I don't have to unpack it. Paul is so anxious you should not misunderstand what he means about salvation that he actually invents three words in Ephesians 2 so that you can understand.

The first is in verse 5. I'll have to say it as lots of English words, but you'll have to take my word for it; it's one word as Paul creates it: 'made us alive together with Christ'. The second word that Paul invents is in verse 6: 'raised us up together with Christ'. And the third is also in verse 6: 'made us sit together with Christ'.

Imagine the apostle Paul is rather intrigued about the Keswick Convention; he's rather distressed about our Christian teaching in the United Kingdom, so he comes to the Keswick platform and says, 'I want to just run through a few basic truths with you to see how you understand God's truth. Hands up those that can tell me where we are outside Christ.'

Well, we all know that, so we put up our hands and we say, 'Paul, we're dead in our trangressions and sins.'

Paul says, 'OK. Well, where are we *in* Christ?'

'Well,' we reply, 'at the moment we're in Keswick in Cumbria.'

'No, no,' Paul says; 'let me put it another way. Think of the things that have historically happened to Jesus since He died. Can someone tell me what those are?'

Someone dares to put up their hand, and he points to

them. 'Well, there was resurrection; He rose on that first Easter day.'

'Right,' says Paul; 'what else?'

Somebody else puts their hand up and says, 'There was ascension; He returned to heaven.'

Only the Scots can produce the third theological word, that rhymes with resurrection and ascension, because they use it in their church life. But it's a theological word: 'session'. It means being seated in the place of ruling and authority.

So Paul asks again: 'Where are we outside Christ?'

We put up our hands and say, 'Paul, if we're outside Jesus Christ, we're dead in our transgressions and sins.'

'OK,' says Paul; 'where are we *in* Christ?'

'Oh, we see what you're getting at, Paul. You mean that if we are in Christ, exactly the same things that have happened to Christ have happened to us.'

'Precisely,' says Paul. 'That is the gospel of Jesus Christ. Outside Him you're dead, but if you're in Him you've been made alive together with Him. You've been raised together with Him and you are seated together with Him in the heavenlies.'

John Stott says in his commentary, 'If the Christian community are seated with Christ, there is no doubt about the objects upon which they are sitting; they're sitting on thrones.'

The marvellous, the beautiful building of the community of God! God *starts* His marvellous community and God *shapes* His marvellous community, and that's all so that God can *show* His marvellous community.

God shows His marvellous community

We find this in verse 6. The only reason we haven't been taken to heaven today is that God wants us to remain here as a walking, talking, visual aid of redemption.

A little while ago I was preaching an evening series of

sermons. We were free during the day and my wife said that she would like to go and see the Chagall exhibition at the Royal Academy in London, so we went. We saw the exhibition, and as we came out of the Royal Academy I turned left to go to Piccadilly Tube Station. Hazel said, 'The sun is shining this way; could we walk this way for a moment?' And then, as we walked a few feet along Piccadilly, 'Let's walk down Old Bond Street.'

You know what was happening to me. I was being taken shopping and I hadn't realised it! We managed to get by Gucci's and Cartier's. At Asprey's the jewellers they had something in their window rather like an elephant, about the size of a pineapple, and it was leaping out of the window saying, 'Buy me! How have you managed to live for fifty-seven years without me? Price £2,000.'

The next window was full of silver-plated tongs for getting the tea-bag out of a cup of tea. I had to step back, and I read the sign saying 'Jewellers to Her Majesty Queen Elizabeth II'. I thought, 'Why can't she use a pencil like everybody else?' £70 for silver-plated tongs! Well, we survived.

Bond Street is really just like any high street. Things are leaping out of the windows and saying, 'Buy me, buy me.' And we, likewise, are God's walking, talking advertisements for redemption. That's why it's important that our lives are seen to change.

Isn't it marvellous what has happened in the last few weeks, as the solid structure of the Berlin Wall has come down and the people of Eastern Europe are free? What Paul is trying to say here is that the Iron Curtain between this world and heaven is coming down and spiritually we're free, we're in Christ.

A little while ago we were staying with somebody and I had one of those sleepless nights that you get occasionally, and I couldn't sleep. So I started to read Charles Dickens's *The Tale of Two Cities*. I couldn't put it down.

You probably know the story. An Englishman is freed from the Bastille after many years. He returns to his mansion in England; he enjoys the freedom, he loves the smell of the fresh grass, loves the feel of the sunshine. But after a while it all palls on him, and he says to his manservant, 'I want to build a stone room, here in the sitting room, about five-foot six high and five-foot wide with a space for a door in it.'

And when the stonemason has built it, he gets the blacksmith in to put an iron door on it with a padlock and a sliding window at the bottom where things can be put in. And when that's done, the master of the house calls his servant and says, 'Look, this is the key; I know that you'll think this is odd, but I've been so long in a cell that I don't feel comfortable with all this freedom. Would you take the key and when I'm in there, lock the door? If you can put bread and water in several times a day, that's marvellous. If you can find people that need shoes to be repaired, put them in and I will repair them, but don't let me out. Here's the key. I'm going to step into the little cell. Oh, I can't tell you how much better this feels! I feel at home in here. Will you lock the door?'

Do you know, when I read that, I said that describes the Christian church in my land today? Outside Christ we're dead in our transgressions and sins. If we're in Christ, of course we're going to battle with sin, every day of our lives, but we can begin to enjoy the victory and the life that Christ has for us. If we're in Christ we've been made alive together with Christ, we've been raised together with Christ, we're seated together with Christ in the heavenlies.

'Oh God, I don't like spiritual maturity or freedom. Can I go back to where I was before?'

Paul says, 'My brother, my sister, it cannot happen. You're either outside Christ and dead, or you're in Him. Yes, it's a battle; yes, it's a struggle; but you've been made alive together with Him, you've been raised together with Him, you're seated together with Him in the heavenlies.' And we should be walking tall as God's redeemed people.

Have you been born again of the Spirit yet, or you're here with a friend and you haven't become committed to Christ? Are you trying to get back into the old cell, the place of bondage? You need to step out tonight, to learn to walk tall, to be God's walking, talking visual aid of redemption.

You've been made alive together with Christ. You're raised together with Christ. You're seated with Him.

LORD OF ALL

by Rev. Philip Hacking

Colossians 1:15–23

We have just listened to the words of the song 'Behold the Man'. And I hope that as you listened you saw that there is no conflict between 'Jesus our Saviour' and 'Jesus our Lord'. For the one who is Lord is the one who was crucified; He is the 'Lamb upon the throne', He is 'Servant'. Blend these together—'Behold the man'. And I guess you remember those words, some of the most remarkable spoken by Pilate; he spoke more than he ever knew: he called Him 'this man . . .'.

But of course it matters that 'the man' was also God. I want you to turn in your Bibles to Colossians 1. Tonight our theme is this great thought: 'Lord of All'.

It is twenty years or more since I last preached at Keswick from the book of Colossians. I spoke from chapter 2—'As you received Christ Jesus the Lord, so walk ye in him.' I turn back to Colossians tonight because here, I believe, is our theme, and not just for tonight: I believe that under God we are this week emphasising the theme of the Majesty of Jesus. It's the theme of our Bible Readings, and in all kinds of ways we are majoring on the person of Jesus Christ. And I believe also that on the day of the Keswick week when we talk about the lordship of

Jesus and people are responding to that message, here we are meant to be.

If you read a commentary on Colossians, you will probably find that the writer spends several pages discussing the 'Colossian heresy'. Now, commentators always enjoy debating things to which they know there's no final answer; it's a lot easier! And so they spend a long time telling us that ultimately they don't know what the Colossian heresy was (it might have been easier if they'd told us so in a few words!).

We don't know what it was, but what we do know about the Colossian heresy is that it diminished the person of Jesus; it brought Him down. In a sense, it was a New Age movement long before its time.

Now what I find tremendous about Paul is his response to heresy. We've been reminded by Michael Baughen that heresy is very much abroad in our churches today—when we are faced with teaching that diminishes Jesus, that makes Him a pint-sized Saviour, not worth giving your life to. Not surprisingly, young people find no fascination in that kind of Jesus. Why should they?

In Colossians, when Paul wants to deal with a heresy that belittles Jesus, what does he do? He doesn't major on the heresy (that's why we don't know what it was). Why? Because he wants his readers to see how great Jesus is. May I just say in passing—do be careful; it's possible to get so fascinated with things like the New Age and the occult and the devil and demons, that in a strange way— the devil is very subtle—we become so fascinated with the things we condemn that they creep in by the back door. And there are signs that the New Age has its movements in the church. If so, be careful.

Be careful that you're not allowing the devil in by the back door, by your fascination about what you condemn.

Make much of Jesus, fill your life with Him, get Him where He ought to be in your life. Then we've got something not merely to measure up to the New Age but to overcome it. We don't fear a 'New Age', because we have the one who's ever new, who is a sovereign Lord. And when the church recaptures that, we have nothing to fear.

So here in Colossians Paul prays for these Christians he's never met. You see, he doesn't just want them to be good orthodox theologians. There could be people in this tent at Keswick who believe that Jesus is *the* man and that He is the Son of God, but for whom it hasn't made much practical difference. You might even sing great hymns about lordship and consecration, but when it comes to the pinch and the chips are down, you're not offering your life. You may believe it in theory—but 'don't ask me to do anything about it'.

Paul prays for these Colossian Christians. Look at your Bible (verse 9 onwards). He tells them what he is praying for. He's praying that they might be wise, that they might be consistent, that they might have the power of God, that they might be delivered (verse 13). And as He rejoices at the deliverance wrought by the Redeemer, He goes on to the glory of the Redeemer. Always remember, you can't have the glory of the Redeemer if He is only '*a* man'. But if He is '*the* man', then all this is possible.

Two phrases stand out in our passage. Verse 15: He is 'the image of the invisible God'. Verse 19: it's difficult grammatically, but it seems to say, 'God was pleased to have all his fullness dwell in him.' In a sense they are saying the same thing, that Jesus is God whom we can understand. We saw it in our studies in Hebrews 1. He is God in the image that we can know. What is man? Made in the image of God. So when Paul says He's the image of the invisible God, he is also saying He is really man as man was meant to be.

And He is also God as we can understand. Verse 19 speaks of all the fullness of God in Him; and Jesus dared to say, 'Whoever has seen me has seen the Father.'

Shortly after the Keswick Convention we go to the Cotswolds for a fortnight's holiday. When we get back, the count-down to Christmas is under way. Now: unless it is true that we believe Jesus to be the God-man, we do a lot of nonsense at Christmas, we really do. But if we really believe that 'Lo within a manger lies, He who built the starry skies'...

Go on to Easter. People of my generation often sing, ''Tis mystery all, the Immortal dies...' Have you thought what that means? And if you belong to a more modern generation, listen to these words of Graham Kendrick! 'Hands that flung stars into space, to cruel nails surrendered.' Please, older people, never despise modern hymns. It worries me that some of us are so set in our ways. I don't think Wesley ever wrote anything more beautiful than that. But whether you are Wesley or Kendrick, isn't it amazing that what we are actually saying is that there on a cross, there was not just a man setting an example—there was God Himself. And only because it was God Himself, could we be redeemed.

Now on the back of all that Paul wants to say to us, as to these Colossians, as we face a heresy that is sweeping our country and demands Christians who believe in the lordship of Christ and live by the light of it—he is saying to us, 'Do you believe He is Lord? Are you prepared for the consequences?'

Lord of creation

First of all (verses 15–17), He is Lord of creation. Note three little pregnant phrases: 'by him', 'in him', 'for him'.

By Him

He is the firstborn over all creation (verse 15). Seven times Paul talks about 'all things', 'everything'. Do you see the wonder of it? We have been reminded about those 'octillions' of stars. I've been pondering that marvellous mathematical phrase ever since! And there's a lovely passage in Genesis 1, almost a throw-away line: 'He made the stars also'—while He was at it, He made octillions of stars also. Who did? Well, Jesus did. The second person of the Trinity is the agent of creation.

The sovereign Lord is sovereign over all things. What is more important, He is sovereign over all that is happening in providence and in history, not just over creation. It's a tremendous theme! May I ask you to believe in creation, not in environment. There is a difference. The environment makes us—makes this planet—the centre. Creation says, 'No: God is the centre.'

Of course we care about the created world. We are all 'green' nowadays, and that's good up to a point. But it's creation, not environment, that is our priority. God is sovereign, and He may choose to end it all on this planet. And what is affecting it is man's sin, and only Christians can get that across.

Do I honestly believe that He's got the whole world in His hand, that He's got the tiny little baby in His hand? For that's what Scripture's saying.

In the New Testament there is a verb used about the cross: 'God delivered him [that is, Jesus] for us all.' The word 'delivered' is the very same word that is used for what Judas did, Pilate did and the Jews did. Do you see the marvel of it? They did it for treachery, they did it out of fear and out of hatred. But God was doing it to work out our full salvation. The greatest sin in human history became the greatest agent of good. 'Where sin abounded grace did much more abound' (Romans 5:20). If I believe that, then in my life I can believe that He does work all things together for good by Him.

In Him

Secondly (verse 17), 'In him all things hold together.' It is what the experts call the principle of coherence; it means that in Christ things hold together. It is like the central cryptic clue in a crossword puzzle, the one that, when you solve it, makes everything else fit together. Have you yet found that all things hold together in Christ? It should be true for you and for me, and if it is true for us, then it is something that we want to say to the contemporary world: that we shall never discover peace, unity and hope, until we find Christ in the centre.

I remember a senior medical man in my congregation telling a group of us, for prayer, that he had been at a gathering of senior medics where they had been discussing some of the problems of AIDS. And he dared to suggest that if only people followed the clearly written biblical instructions about sex, we would solve most of the problems. He was hounded out as being intolerant, unjust and unscientific; but he was right. And if our world will not obey the Maker's instructions, it will not hold together. You know it, I know it. Yes, we proclaim it; but let's proclaim it, believe in it and live by it. 'In him all things hold together.'

You see, the lordship of Christ is much, much more than people today giving their lives to Christian service. It includes that, but it means a lot more. It's a message for the world. 'In him'.

For Him

The third phrase comes at the end of verse 16. 'All things were created by him and for him.' The Greek is quite clear: 'unto him'. It is a goal we're going towards.

They've sent a telescope into space to find out how

things began. (I don't know why they bothered; I could have told them, it would have saved a lot of money.) But they'll never send anything up into space to find out how it's all going to end. I used to love Dr Who. We can't project ourselves into space as he could. But Scripture says that we know creation has a goal. Read Romans 8:18–21, which talks about creation on tiptoe waiting for the revealing of the sons of God, waiting for that great day, and Christians groaning within themselves with creation, waiting for that day.

And we move towards Christ; He is the agent, He is the preserver, He is the goal—'Until Christ one day returns'. We never know when we shall reach that goal. What we do know is that we are moving, and that's what the world doesn't know; and there's nothing more hopeless and helpless.

I took two funeral services within a matter of days. One was a marvellous thanksgiving service; the other only a week before, where there was no hope or faith. So I preached the gospel to them. But you see, there was all the difference in the world, and all the difference in eternity, between the two funerals. And no philosophy, no religion apart from Christ, gives any assurance or hope. But we know we're going to Christ, the Lord of Creation. He is Lord.

Lord of the church

Secondly (verses 18–20), He is Lord of the church. Would you please note a small difference here, for it says in verse 18 literally 'that in everything he might become supreme'. Now I don't understand this fully. We saw in Hebrews that marvellous word about Jesus learning obedience through the things He suffered; that Jesus has always been the eternal Son of God, but He has become something more; and in a sense, in heaven now He is even greater than before.

I hope that's not heresy, I think it's true; because in heaven He's taken manhood, He's taken into heaven the marks of the cross, and He's become Lord of the church; in two ways.

Through reconciliation

We are reminded in verse 20 that it was God's pleasure to reconcile to Himself all things through the blood of Christ shed on the cross. Note, it's 'all things', not 'all men'. There's no way that you can make the Bible say that all men will be reconciled to God, that at the end of the day we are all there. That, of course, the Bible does not say.

And probably every single one of us believes that in theory; but it doesn't move us to evangelise as if we did believe it. If the thousands who came to Keswick really were fired with the belief that there's an eternal division, oh! what a difference it would make to evangelism.

I recollect preaching here years ago shortly after a great meeting in the Sheffield city hall, and I felt quite aggrieved. Richard Wurmbrand had spoken to thousands of people there, it was packed to the door. We listened to him talk about his sufferings. Everybody was moved. Being a man to seize any opportunity, and knowing that we were all moved at the account of a Christian's suffering, I announced from the platform that we intended to visit people in the city who were outside Christ.

'It's going to be costly; are you ready?'

I think I got half a dozen volunteers out of 2,500. And I went away a disillusioned man. Oh, they thought that it was marvellous that a man should suffer, they wept with him, they thought he was wonderful, and they sang their hymns and shook his hand. But ask them to walk up some steps and knock on a door, and talk to people without Christ—they're lost. I would have thought that more than half a dozen out of 2,500 might have had the courage. And bless Sheffield, it's neither worse nor better than many places.

Verse 20 doesn't say, 'Things in earth and things in heaven and things under the earth', as does Philippians 2. It's a reminder of the reality of hell. There is a Judgement Day, and the day will come when everybody will acknowledge Jesus is Lord, but some will do so in fear and trembling.

And please, remember the cost; what it cost the man on the cross to shed His blood. And then, think that it wasn't just a man going through the agonies of physical suffering. It was the Son of God, separate from God whom He'd known from all eternity, crying to a dead heaven, 'My God, My God, why...?' And think of God the Father in heaven shutting His ears because He knew He couldn't do anything to rescue Jesus His Son. That's the cost.

If I had more time I would point out to you that it's not only a matter of reconciling us to Him, but of reconciling Him to us (cf. Romans 3); that God is a Judge, a just God, and that in one sense He too needs to be reconciled. He always loves us but He's a holy God, and only the death of a God-man on the cross could make it possible, through reconciliation.

Through resurrection
Through resurrection He is Lord of the church. He is the firstborn from the dead (verse 18). You might think it was not so; there were at least two people in the Old Testament raised from the dead, and Jesus Himself raised Jairus, and the widow of Nain's son, and Lazarus. So how is Jesus different?

They were all going to die again. It was no kindness to Lazarus that He raised him from the dead. I often wonder if that's why Jesus wept, that He had to bring him back from the dead as a sign. After all, poor Lazarus had to go

through dying twice. But Jesus, raised from the dead,
would never die again. He is the firstborn from the dead.
And because He is that, He is Lord of the church and we
may know the resurrection power.

That is tremendous. But the challenge crosses all
denominational boundaries. Is Jesus Lord? Is that really
true? For it might affect the way we work and the way we
worship, if He really were Lord, the Head of the church.
He is the Bridegroom—that tremendous picture!—and
we are the bride. He is the Head, we are the body. He is
the Foundation, we are the building.

Sometimes, when the church begins to be strong, it
loses sight of the essentials. I was very humbled just over a
year ago to preach in Korea to thousands of people. And
they asked me to say what I thought about the church in
Korea, and what I thought about its future. Now, who am
I? And when I think about the level of church-going in
England, who dare say anything about those magnificent
thousands of people?

But I did dare say this, since they asked me, and I
didn't just want to say pleasantries. I said that here was a
church that had flourished, that had grown. It was alive,
large, wealthy. I said, 'Be careful. There was a time when
the church in England was like that (though we never had
quite such enormous congregations). It isn't now. Why
not? Because somewhere along the line we lost sight of
the authority of Scripture and the sovereignty of Jesus,
and so at the moment of our apparent strength we began
to dwindle.'

I dared to say to them, it could happen in Korea. And I
want to tell you that one or two Korean pastors in positions of leadership were gracious enough to thank me and
say, 'You're right, it could be beginning already.' The
Korean church is a marvellous church, from which we've a
lot to learn. But I want to say that if *any* church, however

strong it may seem to be, loses sight of the lordship of Jesus, then when that happens, it begins to decline.

F.F. Bruce tells a story of the pre-Reformation Catholic Church. I repeat it because it could be true of any church. The Pope and a cardinal were discussing Acts 3, the healing of the lame beggar. Peter, you remember, said, 'Silver and gold have I none. What I have I give you. In the name of Jesus, rise and walk.' And the Pope said to the cardinal, 'We don't have to say "Silver and gold have I none" any more.' And the cardinal said, 'No—and that's perhaps why we can no more say, "In the name of Jesus rise and walk." '

Ponder it. It can happen anywhere. Is Jesus Lord of the church? Yes. But is He acknowledged as such?

Lord of my life

Finally, 'Lord of my life'. For Paul moves, in verse 21, from the cosmic Jesus to the personal Saviour. But never forget He *is* the cosmic Jesus. Don't diminish Him. He is Lord of your life because He is Lord of creation and Lord of the church. To regard Him as our personal Saviour does not make Him any less. Indeed, maybe it's more trouble to Him to look after your life and mine than after all creation!

The first two words in verse 21 are, in the Greek, 'And *you*'. So I want you to think through in these last few moments, 'Is He Lord of my life?'

Three beautiful thoughts come out here. First of all,

Saving me
Once you were alienated in your minds and your behaviour. You were enemies (1:21). Yes—that's true of all of us. 'But now'—this is one of those great 'but nows'—'he has reconciled you by Christ's physical body through death.' So He's saved me—that lovely old word.

He is Lord of my life in saving me. Well, I guess there are
some in Keswick who haven't even got there. And I
wonder whether tonight you'll get to that place where you
want to say: 'Oh the man, my Saviour, I need Him, there's
no other way.'

Sanctifying me

Why has He reconciled me? Verse 22: 'To present you
holy in his sight, without blemish and free from accusa-
tion.' That's a lovely picture; the purpose of Christ's saving us is that He might sanctify us, so that one day He will
present us glorified before His Father. When He is Lord
of our lives He changes us. And that's the thrill of being a
Christian. It's a continuing process, so that one day He
might present us without blemish.

'Without blemish'—it's a picture of Jesus; the Lamb of
God without blemish and without spot. And in one sense,
what Paul is saying is that Jesus wants to make us the
perfect sacrifice. And one of the great marks of Keswick
down the years is that the theme of holiness must always
be matched with the theme of service.

Holiness without service can be a cloistered virtue, and
service without holiness can be very superficial. Some
want to be active, but aren't progressing in the life of
holiness. Some are happy to talk about holiness, but
aren't ready for service. Here's the picture of a sacrifice.
Please note (verse 23, linking beautifully with what Michael Baughen has been saying to us from Hebrews): 'He is
going to do all this if you continue in your faith.' God
ordains the means as well as the end.

The perseverance of the saints—a great doctrine in
which I absolutely believe—doesn't so much say that if
you're a saint you'll persevere, as that if you persevere
you're a saint. If you continue with God, then you'll grow
in holiness. It's not we who've chosen Him but He who
has chosen us; but we have to respond.

Thank God, none can ever pluck us out of His hand. But are we safe and secure in that hand? Jesus said, 'Not everyone who says "Lord, Lord" shall enter, but he who does the will of my Father.'

Saving me He is Lord; sanctifying me He is Lord. Yes, it's the work of the Holy Spirit, but it's Jesus' work as well. It's His work to set us apart, to sanctify us by His Spirit. Saving me, sanctifying me.

Strengthening me

Verse 23: 'Established and firm, not moved from the hope held out in the gospel. The gospel you heard has been proclaimed to every creature under heaven.' Do you know, I think Paul is guilty of an exaggeration there! Do you really think the gospel's been preached to every creature under heaven? But in that little phrase, Paul is saying to the Christians in Colosse, 'You are not alone. The gospel's going throughout the world. And that gospel is bearing fruit and all.' What a challenge!

You see, if I do believe that the gospel is still to be preached to every creature under heaven (and that means as much to people in high-rise flats in Sheffield as to people in high-rise flats in Hong Kong) then maybe part of my holiness must be my willingness to serve. There is no blessing apart from sacrifice. Work that one out! And for Jesus the man, the way to glory had to be the way of the cross.

One of our congregation ministering in Nepal wrote to us, 'It's the birthright of every Christian here to go to prison.' Exaggeration? Well, perhaps, like Paul; but there's a lot of truth in it. And the Lord is saying to some of us that if He's Lord of our life, then we must be ready for that.

And here's the joy of it: 'If I continue in you'—and that may mean a willingness to step out in faith—'then I shall be established firm, not moved from the hope.' You cannot dissociate the two. If you want to be the kind of Christian who sits back and says, 'Isn't it a lovely Christian hope, a hope for the world; and I can enjoy life and sit back and luxuriate in it!'—then you haven't got the message.

'Go and make disciples; and lo I am with you always.' The best place for becoming more like Jesus is to dare to take up your cross and follow Him.

We come towards the end.

A few years ago I was rebuked by a reverend gentleman because we sang a particular modern chorus here. He was quite right. We no longer sing, 'Jesus we enthrone You, Jesus take Your place.' Jesus is *already* enthroned, He's already taken His place. We don't make Jesus Lord, He *is* Lord. And I thank my theologian friend for putting me right.

But here's my big 'But'. Is there a danger, because we know we cannot make Him Lord, of failing to *acknowledge* Him as Lord, and failing to *obey* Him as Lord in that place where He's speaking to us tonight? Is He Lord over what you do with your money, over your marriage relationship, over what you do with your time, over work in the church? Is He Lord over your willingness to say, 'I am ready to go wherever and whenever He may call me'?

No, you can't enthrone Him, He is Lord already. But do you obey Him?

THE SPIRIT'S GIFT FOR OTHERS

by Mr Billy Strachan

1 Corinthians 12:27–31

The ministry of the Spirit in the life of a believer

I believe in the Holy Spirit. But it's the Spirit who is Holy. Too often today that third person of the Godhead is referred to simply as 'the Spirit', and too few remember to give Him His designation, that He is a *Holy* Spirit; because if we reminded ourselves, by doing so, we may get a fresh glimpse of the kind of life that we should be living if we claim to be indwelt by Him.

I believe in the *fullness* of the Holy Spirit, not just once, but regularly; and I believe in the *gifts* of the Holy Spirit, all of them. And as I read through the chapters in Corinthians regarding the subject for this evening, my eye lighted on a text that I thought I would not have gone to, and it's 1 Corinthians 14:19: 'Yet in the church I had rather speak five words with my understanding, that by my voice I might teach others also, than ten thousand words in an unknown tongue.'

I don't know what the five words were that Paul had in mind, but I sat and thought to myself, 'What would I choose to be the five words that I would like to say—that would be a means of edifying the body, rather than simply having some ecstatic blessing and edification for myself in ten thousand unknown words?'

The five words that came to my mind (and several sets of five did, and it was difficult deciding which to choose) were these: 'What gift do you want?' I stared at that for some time in my thought processes, and then up came my second five: 'What gift did you get?' So I thought, 'Perhaps I should address my remarks on that five,' when another five jumped into mind: 'What gift do you need?'

And I thought, 'Well, it's got to be one of those,' when I was surprised by the intrusion of another five, mainly addressed to those believers among us who already know that they do possess the gifts of the Spirit. And these words were, 'What good did it do?'

You have a gift, confirming within you the presence of the Holy Spirit in your heart and life, adding to your assurance that He's there. To what end? What good did that gift do in your personal life? Was it simply for self-satisfaction, or has it been utilised extensively and regularly under the control of the person of the Holy Spirit, to be a blessing wherever you are in every twenty-four hours of every day?

I'm always amused when I hear people talk about the gifts of the Spirit, and the argument that goes on about which should be the most important. I don't know if you've studied the gifts of the Spirit in Corinthians, but if you do so you'll discover that there are two lists. The first list is to do with benefiting yourself, and the other is for you to be a benefit to others.

I've often told my students that if someone marched to the lectern of the Bible school and put a gun to my forehead and said, 'Strachan, you just have thirty seconds left to give a last-minute message to your students before we pull the trigger; what is the message you would like to give to your students?', I've only one word I would shout without hesitation to them before the trigger was pulled and it's this: 'Others!' Then I would go to be with the Lord, content.

A careful study of the ministry of the Spirit in Scripture will bring out to your heart, as it has to mine, that He's there with all that He is within you, to equip you to be a blessing to others, never simply to be self-satisfied that you're full. It's always surprised me, when reading the list of the gifts that make you a blessing to others, that people underline the evangelist, the pastor, the teacher; but, you know, there's one in there that I love, and it is the gift of 'helpers'.

I don't know why we don't make that *the* criterion for being indwelt by the Spirit. I don't know why they pick the others, because from what I've observed some people are no help to anyone.

Thank God, as I go through my Bible I find a woman with a tent-peg and a hammer. And they say there's no place for women in the ministry! She did more in changing the events of Israel's history with that tent-peg and hammer and the ability to cook a hot cup of milk, than anyone else in Scripture.

Thank God for the man who was simply an athlete! He could outrun a liar about to take a wrong message to a king, and change the course of history.

Thank God for a left-handed misfit called Ehud! I know you wouldn't have him on your short-list as a speaker in your church; you wouldn't know how to introduce him. And yet he was a man that changed the course of history.

And thank God for a couple that had a spare bedroom and let the prophet stay there any time he passed through!

They were helps; a great means of helping. What good did it do? Are you a help?

I often ask the students, when studying the passage in Galatians, when it states that 'when the fullness of the

time had come' Christ entered the world (4:4), 'Why do
you think that particular moment out of all history, was
the fullness of time for Him to come?' The sort of answer I
get back is: 'Well, sin was so rampant, the pagans were
progressing, permissiveness was getting terrible, and
unless the Lord had come to convert these awful sinners,
nothing would have happened.'

I reply 'You're all wrong!' Read the last book of the
Old Testament and you find that God was getting tired of
the believers. 'You weary me,' He said. God has feelings.
How do I know? Because you've got them, and you're
made in the image of God, and what you feel is minute
compared to how He feels.

How often we say to people, 'You just make me tired!'

And by the end of the Old Testament, the Almighty
God said to His people, 'You just make Me tired!' (cf.
Malachi 2:17). They answered Him back. 'When did we
ever make You tired? We've never missed an opportunity
to be at the temple, say our prayers, go through the
routine.'

He said, 'You've robbed me in tithes and offerings.'

'No—ask the treasurer; I give.'

Do you know the easiest part of Christianity these
days? Giving cash—and not give yourself. If you go back
and do a study of the tithing in the Old Testament you'll
discover to your amazement that there was more than the
tenth. That was the temple tax. There was a tax for self
and for your family, but there was also a tithe of your
time, your life, your everything, for others; the poor, the
needy, the stranger.

And Malachi mentions it. The fatherless and the
widows—no one was helping them. And isn't it interesting that stodgy old James, in his practicality—no wonder
people don't like his epistle—gives us a practical definition of true religion? I know that we tend to be down on

religious people that are not born again, but there is a true religion. And James says this at the end of the first chapter: 'If any man among you seem to be religious'—and in the next verse: 'Pure religion and undefiled before God and the Father is this...'—you don't have to guess; you don't need a theologian to tell you, it *is* this: '...to visit the fatherless and widows in their affliction' (James 1:26–27).

It has a side benefit. It so occupies you, you don't have time to sin! People often say to me, 'How do you defeat those sins that so easily beset us?' I say, 'Occupy yourself with others; go and be a help.'

Now, it's rather interesting that in James they translated that word 'religion'. But in Greek—and it's the only time it's ever used this way—it's simply the word 'worship'. That's difficult to swallow, because most people's idea of worship is a togetherness of fellowship in a place of worship, having great songs and uplifted hearts and feelings to God in praise and adoration; and James turns round and says, 'I'll tell you what's acceptable worship: getting out there and helping Mrs Jones—people who are fatherless and widows.' Have you ever done that?

The night that Grace and I left for our honeymoon, we made a detour to visit a town, to visit a gentleman who didn't come to the wedding, and we're glad we did because it was only a matter of days before he went to be with the Lord. I didn't return to that town to preach for some time after that, but the next time I was back there I saw his wife enter the church just before the service was due to begin. I committed the unpardonable sin—I left the platform to go down and greet her.

Everybody was looking at the clock and looking at me as much as to say, 'You can't, you've got to start dead on time'—the magic moment of 6.30 on a Sunday evening. But I went down and gave her a hug and said, 'Nice to see you.' Her eyes filled with tears. I said, 'What's the matter?' She said, 'That's the first human touch I've had in this place since George died.'

But she was expected to be there every Sabbath day; because what would dear George think if he looked over the battlements of heaven and she wasn't in the rightful place on a Sunday being faithful? But nobody had ever said, 'Would you like to come round for tea? Are you getting the coal in all right? Do you want a help with the groceries?' Yes, but of course that would mean maybe losing an episode of *Neighbours*, wouldn't it; and you'd miss the continuation of the story...

I was intrigued recently when rereading the parables of the kingdom, how Christ concluded all His teaching about His kingdom in a way that I would never have concluded *my* teaching on the kingdom, if I had been the King writing about my kingdom. I would have certainly started as He started in Matthew 13, with the sowing of the kingdom, the growing of the kingdom. I would have gone through each of the teachings that He taught, just as He did. But it was such an anti-climax when you got to the end. I would have written, 'I'm the King of the castle— and you're all a bunch of dirty wee rascals!'

But have you ever studied the last parable of the kingdom—before He went out to get on with the dignity of dying on a cross for the sin of the whole world? He said, 'I'm going to be setting people at my right and on my left, and I will be saying to those on my right, "Enter ye into the joy of your Lord, you good and faithful servant." '

And they'll be looking rather surprised and saying, 'Us? Have you got the right list? Must be some mistake; couldn't be me. I was never an evangelist, a teacher, a preacher, a lay-worker. They wouldn't even let me do the coffee cups! Must have got the wrong one!' And He'll respond, 'I was hungry and you fed Me; I was thirsty, and you gave Me something to drink; I was a stranger, and you took Me in; naked, and you clothed Me; sick, and you visited Me; I was in prison, and you came unto me.'

There's not a word in there about being a preacher, a teacher, an evangelist. They were *helpers*.

When I was in hospital myself a few years back, just recovering from an operation, a lady with her little son of about seven or eight came in opposite me to visit her husband. I knew Grace wouldn't be coming in the afternoon so I didn't expect a visitor. The lady told the little lad to 'Sit up there and mind your own business while I cheer your father up', and she set to cheering the father up in the usual way that wives cheer fathers up in hospital: 'I hope you hurry up and get out—the roof's leaking, the grass is waiting to be cut, and you've got that other three hundred jobs that haven't been done for a long time'—as she eats his grapes and drinks his juice.

You could see that the little lad was not all that interested in this, and so he was looking around. I was amazed that a child could see it before an adult could, but he looked round all the beds and observed that mine was the only one without a visitor. I heard him say in a stage whisper to his mother, 'Mummy, that poor old man doesn't have a visitor. Do you think I could go and visit him?' And she said, 'Yes, go on while I cheer your dad up.' He came over and said, 'Could I visit you?' And I said, 'Great, pull up a chair.' We got paper out and we drew a lot of ducks and frogs and had a good time. And he said, 'And I'll come back and see you tomorrow.'

Next day he brought me a get-well card he had made himself. 'Unfortunately my daddy's going home today so I doubt if I'll ever see you again,' he said, 'It's been nice to let me be your visitor.' And he gave me a great big hug and a kiss.

It was just at that time something must have fallen in

my eye because I had to turn and look out the window for a time. The hospital was on a hill, and as my eyes cleared I found myself looking down to the town, and suddenly I became very conscious of the fact that I could see the spires of the churches. And I could see where the Brethren met, and the Baptists; the Methodist chapels, the house groups. I knew where they all were because I had spoken in each of them, if not several times in the last twenty to thirty years, at least once each. And I suddenly said to myself, 'I wonder where the Christians are this week?' Of course, it was a silly question to ask; they were probably in another meeting, getting more ready to begin.

Have you ever found that believers who possess Christ—who can only be in them through the presence of the Holy Spirit, who has got the authority and the will and the determination to gift you with gifts to fit you to be a blessing to the community—are still constantly trying to get ready to begin, instead of using it all?

That's why He bore down on my thinking with these five words: you have a gift; *what good did it do*?

When you go down from Keswick, is it to your normal worship routine and the great times of fellowship with yourself, or is there a sense in which, for once, without becoming a pastor, a preacher, an evangelist, those of you could use that one gift and be very active in ministry and have a far healthier, blessed year by being a help to others?

Just in closing, have you ever noticed Paul's commendation of a family at the end of his epistle to the Corinthians? We read these words in 1 Corinthians 16:14: 'Let everything be done with love. I beseech you, brethren; you know the house of Stephanas.' He didn't say, 'Do you know?' If you went to Corinth, if you entered the city, stopped anybody in the street and asked, 'Excuse me, I am looking for the house of Stephanas,' they'd say, with a smile, 'Yes, we know where that is.'

What was it that made the house of Stephanas so special? He was the first-fruits of Achaia. 'He was one of the first converts,' says Paul, 'that I had in that community.'

But here is why they were so well-known in the district: 'They have addicted themselves to the ministry of the saints.'

Do you know that that's the only place in the whole of the New Testament where the word is translated 'addicted'? Thirty years ago we wouldn't have bothered with a word like that. It would have meant nothing; but we do know what it means now, because our land is beginning to be riddled with those who are addicted; they're addicted to drugs. We have another slang-word we use in Britain for that kind of people, and that is 'they're hooked'. They just can't get through another day without it. They'll rob, they'll steal money—anything just to be able to get one more needle-full, to have another fix, because 'I just can't live another twenty-four hours without getting another shot; I'm hooked; I just have to have it.'

Do you know what the commendation was of the house of Stephanas? They were hooked on service; they were hooked on being a blessing to others; they were hooked on helping.

Are you hooked? As a person indwelt by Christ through the Holy Spirit, have you an addiction—you just can't go through another day without allowing the Spirit of God to use you to be a help to somebody?

You all said 'Amen' this morning to the blessings of the reality of what Christ has done for us, at the end of the Bible Reading. But can I ask you this evening—How would you like to get hooked?

AN EYE TO THE ROOT

by Rev. Michael Wilcock

Hebrews 12:15

There are two significant letters that you'll see all over
Keswick throughout the summer. You can see them all
the way up Helvellyn Street and all the way down Blen-
cathra Street. They are that great British institution *B&B*:
'bed-and-breakfast'.

I think of Hebrews 12:14–17 as the *B&B* paragraph; not
'bed-and-breakfast' but something else, as you'll see in
due course. And I have two quite substantial preliminary
comments to make about those four verses. First about
verses 16 and 17, and then about verses 14 and 15.

I suppose most of the English translations let you down
occasionally. Though I'm using the NIV this evening, I
would have one or two little quarrels with what it says in
verses 16 and 17. I suppose these days people don't really
know what a 'birthright' is. You'll have noticed that the
NIV has 'inheritance rights', but I guess many of us are
familiar with some other translation, the translations
which used to say, 'Esau, for a mess of pottage, sold his
birthright.'

More serious is the potentially misleading rendering of
verse 17: Esau '...for a single meal sold his birthright.

Afterwards, as you know, when he wanted to inherit this blessing, he was rejected'.

It seems to me that the natural way to read those two verses is to identify the birthright with the blessing. Esau sold his birthright, and afterwards when he wanted to inherit this blessing, he was rejected, as if the birthright and the blessing were the same thing.

Now, in a sense of course they were; they were the two sides of the same coin. But there should really be the word 'the' in front of 'blessing'. And if you've got your Bible open in front of you, read it with that alteration and see what the different emphasis is.

I think the writer of the letter to the Hebrews deliberately distinguishes between the birthright and the blessing, even though in one sense they belong inextricably together. He is talking about two separate incidents. In chapter 25, we read how Esau traded his birthright in exchange for food. And then Genesis separates from that incident the later one in chapter 27, concerning the blessing—which might well have been years afterwards, when in the mind of Esau—though not in the mind of Jacob—the incident about the birthright was long forgotten. And I believe we're meant to read the story that way.

Genesis actually separates the two by an entire chapter talking about something else. Esau for a single meal sold his *birthright*, despising it, thinking nothing of it; afterwards—and maybe it was long, long afterwards, when any connection between the two things had disappeared from the mind of Esau—when he wanted to inherit the *blessing*, to his vast surprise, he found himself rejected.

Now, I make that point as a preliminary because I think it's very important. Bear it in mind, I'll come back to it later. That's still just a preliminary—my first preliminary!

The second preliminary concerns verses 14–15. Verse 14

says to me 'Keswick', and verse 15 says to me 'Convention'.

You ask what I mean by that. The great word 'holiness', there at the heart of verse 14, is in one way what the Keswick Convention is all about. Keswick means holiness. It is the pursuit of the holy Christian life. It is those who seek the Lord and want to live His kind of life, those who want to be the kind of people He wants them to be, those who seek that special, distinctive, righteous, godly way of life, who come to Keswick, because they know that that is where that message is preached.

'Follow after holiness, pursue holiness, without which no-one will see the Lord,' says Keswick—and that's verse 14. But verse 15 says, 'Now see to it', and that's a very interesting word in the Greek; it's the same word from which our word 'bishop' comes.

What is a bishop? A bishop is one who is supposed to oversee the welfare of the people of God. And what the writer of the letter to the Hebrews is saying to us is— 'Now, I want all of you, all who listen to these words, to realise that it's incumbent upon every one of you to see to it that a bit of bishoping is done in all directions, as you come together as a group of people.'

Because when we come to Keswick it is a convention, it is a gathering; it is not just individuals meeting with God. It is that, certainly, and for very many of us, I have no doubt at all, this week will be a time when we as individuals have a personal confrontation with the Lord. But even so, I was part of a convention, I was part of a great congregation, and I came from another congregation back at home, where again I am part of a group of people.

And Hebrews is telling me that it is my responsibility to see to it not simply that I am right with the Lord and seeking the holy life He wants me to live, but that my brothers and my sisters likewise have a thirst after righteousness and a desire for holy living.

That's why we come together. And I hope very much that in the course of this Convention we will not be saying simply as individuals, 'Lord, bless me', but that we shall be praying for one another and saying, 'Lord, the blessing I want for myself, I pray You'll give to my neighbour as well, to all these other folk who are sitting around me in this tent tonight, to the many who will listen to the tapes and watch the videos. Lord, bless them all.' It is my responsibility to see to it that in the great congregation all seek holiness as I seek holiness.

That's why I say that verse 14 says to me 'Keswick', and verse 15 says to me 'the Convention'. It is a gathering together of people who want to see to it that together they will be living a holy life. And that's my second preliminary.

Now I come to the core of what I want to say.

What this paragraph in Hebrews chapter 12 sets before us is an experience of the present. It illustrates that experience by means of an event from the past. The kind of experience that's described in these half-verses is the experience we have nowadays, as God's people always have had all down the ages and no doubt will do to the end of time.

15a: 'See to it that no-one misses the grace of God.' 15b: 'See to it…that no bitter root grows up to cause trouble and defile many.' 16a: 'See [to it] that no-one is sexually immoral or godless.'

'Ah,' you say, 'now he's got to the heart of the sermon, and it's a three-point sermon.' No, you'd be wrong. This is a sermon with a single point, because I believe those three half-verses are all making the same point. 'See to it that no-one misses the grace of God. See to it…that no bitter root grows up. See [to it] that no-one is sexually immoral or godless.'

The story of Esau illustrates that one great point. What the point is, I want to open up for you now.

First of all, the experience with which this passage is concerned. It's put in this way in the first half of verse 15: 'See to it that no-one is falling back from the grace of God.'

The grace of God is leading His people on; it is sufficient for all that we need to live His kind of holy life, and those of us who want to live that kind of life follow hard upon the leading of that grace.

But, says Hebrews 15a, there are certain to be those in your fellowship, in *this* fellowship, who straggle, who fall behind, in the pursuit of that grace. Once they were going on, keeping up with the best of them, but now they're lagging behind. All is not well with them.

Maybe what the half-verse means is, 'See to it that no-one *misses* the grace of God'; that's what the NIV in front of me says. It is as if your first attempts at shooting at that target scored bull's-eye after bull's-eye in those young and enthusiastic days; but increasingly as the time has gone by you don't hit the bull quite so often, you're failing of the grace of God, you're not quite where you should be. And that quest for the holy life is not as realistic or as constant an experience as it once was.

That is a great danger; and it's a constant experience in the churches. Hebrews says, 'See to it that that does not happen. Don't let it happen to yourself; see to it it doesn't happen to those who are near and dear to you, in your own Christian fellowships, that falling back from the grace of God. Let me put it another way,' he says (verse 15b): 'See to it that no bitter root grows up to cause trouble and defile many.'

There were times, no doubt, when you were super-keen, you were newly converted, and you were very sensitive to anything in your life that might not have been quite what God wanted it to be. And you were on it like a terrier on a bone, and you said, 'Out with it!' You took it to the cross of Jesus and you were cleansed from that sin, and you were on the alert all the time.

But now that's not happening so much. Some little root has gone down in your heart, and you haven't noticed it, or if you've noticed it you've ignored it, and it's growing deeper and deeper there. It's going to be harder to pull out later on, but there it is, a root of bitterness that will grow up, and it will cause trouble; and it won't just be to you that it causes trouble, it'll have other effects besides, because you've lost sight of the absolute necessity of keeping short accounts with God, of coming back day by day to the cross of Christ to have that day's sins forgiven.

'Let me put it another way,' says Hebrews (verse 16a). 'See to it that no-one is immoral or godless.' Isn't that fascinating? I believe it's talking about exactly the same sort of thing, because these are above all the two areas in the experience of the believer in which he will find himself, if he's not careful, straggling, falling away from grace, letting a bitter root go down deep in his life.

Why these two particular sins—the immorality that is careless about the kind of person that I am in myself, and the irreligion that is careless about God?

If I'm careless about the way I am deep down inside, maybe nobody else knows about me in those depths. And if I'm careless about my attitude to God and His demands on me, then that bitter thing will take root, and I shall fall away from the grace of God in the sense that this verse means it.

Now, that is the first of my two points. I could say all that, you could hear it all, and we could go home from this meeting somewhat edified, but not actually any the better.

Therefore the letter to the Hebrews drives home the point by illustrating it in such a way that we cannot miss it. Having described that experience which is commonplace—and if we are honest, I think you will join me in saying, 'Yes, that describes me'—here is an event taken out of the distant past of Scripture history to help us to understand what is being said here, this story of Esau, his birthright and his blessing—the *B&B*, which help us to see what it's all about.

Verse 16 is perhaps strange: 'See that no-one is immoral or profane . . .' Some translations put it; 'See that no-one is immoral or profane like Esau.' The commentators say, 'We don't know why it says that, because we know Esau was a profane man but we don't know that he was an immoral man.' What does it mean when it says, 'Don't be immoral or profane like Esau'?

Well, it seems to me that 15a, 15b and 16a are all running in parallel. They all make the same point, of which Esau is the outstanding Bible illustration.

Esau is a man who, as you read his story in Genesis, is falling away from the grace of God (15a). All grace was his. He came at the fountain-head of the story of the people of God. His father was Isaac, his grandfather was Abraham, the father of the faithful; brought up in a godly home, with a godly heritage, all needful grace was his. He had immense privileges. He was a fine man as well with many gifts. And he was lined up for the *B&B*, the birthright and then the blessing. And as the years go by, all those privileges gradually turn sour, and by the end of the story Esau has missed the mark, he's lagged behind, he's out of the race.

Esau is the man to whom verse 15a applies. 'See to it that doesn't happen to you,' says Hebrews.

Let me put it more powerfully. Let me illustrate it. Esau is a man who has a bitter root left in his heart that has never been properly dealt with. And now you come to the separation of those two incidents, one in Genesis 25 and the other in Genesis 27, intended to be separate, as I'm sure they were separated in the mind of Esau—that was the trouble.

No doubt at the time, way back in his youthful days, Esau thought nothing of the birthright and traded it for soup. There was a root of bitterness in the heart of Esau. He was a profane man. But he didn't realise it. It was a tiny thing at the time, small, unperceived, unnoticed, and certainly not dealt with as it should have been dealt with. And time goes by, and the root grows.

Maybe you've got one of the older translations that talks about 'a root of bitterness *springing* up'. I'm sure that's not the right word. The word 'springing' has a suddenness about it, but this wasn't like Jonah's gourd which sprang up overnight. The whole point of this story is that it was a bitter root which had been planted long before, which grew *slowly*. And Esau never realised it was growing.

The years went by, and after a great deal of time, I guess, his father Isaac, the Bible tells us, was old. Then he said, 'Now is the time; I suppose, I may very well be near death. My boys are full-grown. Now's the time to give my eldest son, Esau, the blessing that belongs to the eldest.'

And we all know the story of how Jacob pretended he was Esau, and Isaac gave to Jacob the blessing of the elder son, and Esau came in too late. When he realised what had happened, he cried with an exceeding bitter cry, 'Bless me! Bless me also, my father!' Isaac said, 'But I can't. There was the one blessing for the elder son, and Jacob's got it. I can't do anything about it.'

That was the full tragedy. First of all, it was done for the price of a single meal, a thing that concerned no one but himself and his own stomach. Nobody else, maybe, knew about it except Jacob. One little incident, a private, secret thing, and that was the beginning of the bitter root.

Some of you know the prayer of John Knox, in which he asked for God's forgiveness for all his sins, 'especially for those of which the world cannot accuse me'; the things that no one else knows are wrong in my heart.

But Esau didn't pull up the root. The years pass by, and it's never dealt with, it's never repented, it's never brought to the cross of Christ. In the end, having forfeited the birthright, he loses the blessing as well.

He never made the connection. 'He sought the blessing with tears' (12:17). But he found no place for a change of mind.

Does it mean a change of mind in his father Isaac? 'Isaac, change your mind; give me the blessing instead.' Isaac said, 'I can't change my mind; it's done.'

Or does it mean a change of mind in himself? Oh, he came with many regrets and much remorse, because he'd missed out on the blessing, but he never really found for himself a change of mind, never really repented. Even then, he never really asked for the root to be pulled out. He never really, as we would say, came to the cross.

The thing had had effects, you see; repercussions all down the years. And there were others who suffered because of it afterwards as well. Because of that little private indulgence, when he preferred a bowl of soup to the birthright of the eldest son.

Esau is the man who misses out on the grace of God. He is the man who lets a bitter root grow up to cause trouble and in due course defile every part of his life and other people's lives besides. And Esau is a man who illustrates what immorality or godlessness can do (verse 16a).

To complain that Hebrews has got it wrong, that Esau

may have been an irreligious man but we don't know that he was an immoral man, seems to me to miss the point entirely. That doesn't matter at all. Hebrews is saying that either of these two areas is a danger area for this kind of carelessness. It just so happens that Esau missed out in the God-stakes; it was his relationship to God that was careless. But it might just as well, says Hebrews, have been his relationship to his own inner integrity, his own purity. That would have done just as well, and if he'd failed in both respects it would have been easier still.

Esau is the man who illustrates what either immorality or irreligion—or, still worse, both—can do. Where you and I are careless in either area (maybe many of us know this personally to our cost) we know that that is where the Esau sequence begins.

I'm careless about my attitude to God; I despise the things of God. The cross of my Saviour, Jesus, is set before me, and I am bidden to come there day by day with the sins of that day, and I'm careless about it, and I say, 'Tomorrow will do. It doesn't matter; it's only a little thing; it's a tiny root; it won't grow.' But it will!

Or I'm careless about my inner integrity, about the kind of person I am, and I indulge in things that will compromise that, and I say, 'It's only a little thing; it won't matter; it won't have any effects.' But it will!

Esau stands as a living example of one who embodies that in his own bitter experience. 'The birthright? What good will the birthright do me?' It was the planting of a root that grew and grew and grew, until years later he lost the blessing.

Let me take you back to where we started at the beginning of that paragraph. Verse 14: the great word 'holiness' at the heart of the verse. Verse 15: the great phrase 'see to it', which lies behind both halves of that verse and the beginning of verse 16 as well.

Holiness—see to it!

That is the Keswick Convention's message for us this week. That message is as real and as relevant today as it ever has been. It will never cease to be relevant all down Christian history. When we get to Judgement Day we shall find it has been relevant all the way through. Pursue holiness, the kind of life God wants you to live, day by day. See to it! See to it in your own heart, and see to it in the hearts of those around you in your fellowship.

There has never been a time when the message 'holiness—see to it!' has not been applicable. There has never been a time without the danger of failing the grace of God, there has never been a time when there has not been the danger of letting a little root of evil remain where it is and start to grow. There has never been a time when there has not been the danger of allowing ourselves just a little latitude in that realm of carelessness towards God or towards ourselves, which we call irreligion or immorality. This message is always needed.

You see, there are people nowadays who say, 'This holiness talk is all right for people who are advanced in the Christian life, who are regulars at Keswick, who've been coming for twenty years; they know what it's all about. I'm a very humble Christian. I'm just starting out on the Christian way. That holiness thing is far ahead of me. I'm not like that.'

That 'holiness thing' is for every one of us, however long in the tooth as Christians we may be, however new to the faith we may be. Today the message is 'holiness—see to it'.

Otherwise we're despising the cross of Christ, if we treat sin lightly and say, 'Oh well, these are little things; they don't matter; holiness is something way out there. I'll get there next week. The things I'm doing today don't matter.' They do. And if there is something wrong today, I am to bring it to the cross, and it is to be forgiven today.

There are those who feel they're beyond the cross, and they reckon that because of something they have experienced, some great thing that they believe God has done for them, their usefulness, it seems to them, in God's service, that somehow they're beyond the practical basics of 'holiness—see to it'.

But you can never leave the cross behind. The cross comes forward to you right at the outset of your Christian life, and the cross will pursue you to the very end. And always, always, always you will have to turn back and say, 'Lord, I've failed again; Lord, I've sinned again. How I praise You for the cross which cleanses me again. How I praise You for the grace which forgives me again!' And unless I'm pursuing holiness in that way, the cross of Christ is made of no effect.

Isn't it grand to be reminded, day by day, of the sinfulness of my own heart? It brings me back to my Saviour. Isn't it good to be reminded, day by day, that the goal of holiness still lies ahead of me today, and today I must see to that bitter root, and today I must be careful about those areas of immorality, of irreligion; today I must pursue holiness?

Let's see to it this week, in our own hearts, and let's be praying for one another, that others would be blessed as we want to be blessed.

LOVE'S TARGET

by Rev. Hugh Palmer

1 John 4:14

I want to begin where many versions start a new paragraph, in the middle of 1 John 4:16, with those tremendous three words 'God is love'.

As I was preparing this address, I was talking with some of my friends, and I begged them to stop me ever turning into one of those preachers who can't mention God's love without telling us that 'there's more to God than love'. I know what they mean—particularly in today's usage of the word 'love'—but with some preachers you feel that they begrudge admitting that they have actually got some good news for us! And I'm thrilled with the good news there is in these verses.

'God is love,' John tells us, 'and he who abides in love abides in God, and God abides in him.' That's his great test. John writes his letter not so much to tell us how we can know God, but how we can know that we know Him. And if we're abiding in God and God's abiding in us, why, we can hardly be closer together, can we?

He goes on to say, 'In this is love perfected with us.' It doesn't mean we become flawless. The modern versions have got something like 'made complete'; that's the sense

of the word: 'In this has God's love accomplished its goal';
'In this God's love has reached its target in us'.

You see, John isn't writing us a philosophical essay
about God being love, is he? He's bringing it right down
to our lives and applying it to us, and he says, 'God's love
has reached its target in us.' That's what we're going to
look at tonight.

God's love is designed to give confidence

Here's the first way in which we know when God's love
has reached its target in us. God's love is designed to give
confidence; 'In this is love perfected with us, that we may
have confidence for the day of judgement' (verse 17).
'Courage', the NIV puts it, 'for the day of judgement'; but
the word has behind it the idea of outspokenness, of
freedom of speech.

You know how you can become tongue-tied in some
situations? There are certain people that usually cause it,
aren't there? Almost every family has one relative who
only has to come visiting and you become all tongue-tied.
I was talking to someone the other day about an appalling
situation in her work-place, and she said, 'I know I ought
to speak up, but when they're in the room I just find I
can't say a thing.'

Well, here's the occasion when we're most likely to
shrink back and become tongue-tied, to hang our head in
shame and find we just can't say a thing: the day of
judgement. And John says that God's love is designed
that we might have confidence on that day.

The trouble with verses like these is that we're a little
too familiar with some of those truths; we haven't realised
what an awesome thing it is to have confidence on that
day. Please turn to another writing of John, Revelation 6,
which shows what a staggering truth this is about God's

love. Here's John with his vivid imagery describing that day of judgement, a time when—

> ...the kings of the earth, and the great men, and the generals, and the rich, and the strong, and everyone, slave and free, hid in the caves and among the rocks of the mountains, calling to the mountains and rocks, 'Fall on us and hide us from the face of him who is seated on the throne and from the wrath of the Lamb. For the great day of their wrath has come, and who can stand before it?'
>
> *Revelation 6:15–17*

God's love, John says, is designed to give us confidence on that day. Doesn't that take your breath away? All the great ones and the strong—all those people who are oozing self-confidence now—will cringe. They'll see how empty it is. They won't be able to stand. God's love is targeted to give us confidence then. Have you got confidence for that day?

'How can I have confidence for that day?' Well, come back and see what John has to tell us: 'In this is love perfected with us, that we may have confidence for the day of judgement, because as he is so are we in this world' (4:17).

'As he is so are we'; John writes to the believer. He writes as if we're just like Jesus, that our relationship with the Father is just like His. Do you think Jesus comes cringing and fearful into His Father's presence? Does He have to knock timidly on the door? That's not the way a son comes into a father's presence. Jesus is at His Father's right hand, He's His anointed King.

My son is aged two. He wouldn't dream of knocking before he comes in; it never even occurs to him that I might not want to see him. If he can't open the door, he might try and kick it down, but he certainly wouldn't bother to knock and cringe. And neither need we. As He is, so are we.

Earlier, he has written at the beginning of chapter 3, 'See what love the Father has given us, that we should be called children of God.' But not just called children, for he goes on, 'And so we are.' As He is, so are we.

One more cross-reference, this time to Romans 8, where we see the same truth echoed by Paul. 'When we cry, "*Abba*, Father," ' Paul says, 'it's the Spirit himself bearing witness with our spirit that we are children of God. And if children, then heirs; heirs of God and'— notice this—'heirs of God and fellow-heirs with Christ' (Romans 8:16). You see, we're bracketed right there alongside Him: fellow-heirs with Christ. What He's inherited, so shall we.

'As he is so are we...in this world,' John adds. There are differences. Jesus is in heaven now, and we're not there yet. One of the tensions that goes on between what John has to say and what the opponents are saying in this letter is the issue of in what sense we are like Jesus and in what sense we're not. The opponents seem to want to view themselves as little Christs in every conceivable sense of that word.

John wants to emphasise we're not in heaven yet; the Judgement Day is not behind us but ahead of us. We're not beyond the reach of sin yet—no, not in this world— but we are cleansed from all unrighteousness. There's where we stake our confidence for the day of judgement in 1:9: 'If we confess our sins, he is faithful and just, and will forgive our sins and cleanse us from all unrighteousness.'

I don't think I'll ever forget meeting one middle-aged lady. There seemed good reasons for imagining she'd put her trust in Jesus. She found it very difficult to believe that she was truly forgiven, and after we'd been talking for a while I directed her to that verse. We opened our Bibles and I said to her, 'Now tell me, what is the promise that God makes in that verse?'

She said, 'Well, He promises that He'll forgive our sins and cleanse us from all unrighteousness.'

I said, 'That's right.' Then I asked her, 'What have you done that is not covered by those last two words, "all unrighteousness"?'

She thought for a moment. 'Well, nothing, I suppose.'

I said, 'What's the condition that's attached to this promise?'

She said, 'It says if we confess our sins He'll do that.'

I said, 'Have you confessed your sins to God?'

'Yes.'

I said, 'Are you forgiven, then?'

'Well, I feel some of my sins are forgiven.'

'Do you think God's a liar?' I asked.

'No, no,' she protested. 'Of course He's not a liar.'

'Well, then,' I said, 'what does He promise?'

Well, finally she looked at the verse again and repeated the same answers. We went round once more. 'He promises He'll forgive our sins and cleanse us from all unrighteousness.'

'What have you done,' I said, 'that's not covered by those last two words?'

She knew the questions by now. 'Well,' she said, 'you don't really know what I've done.'

I said, 'No, you're quite right, I don't know anything of what you've done, but I don't need to, do I? What can you possibly have done that's not covered by those last two words? It's pretty all-inclusive, isn't it?'

She agreed.

'Well,' I said, 'what's the condition to the promise?'

She said, 'If we confess our sins.'

'Have you confessed your sins?'

'Yes, I've confessed my sins.'

'Well, are you forgiven, then?'

'Well, I suppose I must be,' she said.

'Yes, I suppose you must be,' I said.

Bit by bit God's love was beginning to reach its target in her, was beginning to penetrate her consciousness, so that she might actually have cause to be confident on the day of judgement, because of one who'd cleansed her from all unrighteousness.

That is love's target. God's love was given that we might have confidence.

Secondly,

God's love was designed to cast out fear

'There is no fear in love. But perfect love casts out fear' (18:4).

Now, understand what John means when he talks of fear. There is a proper fear of God that we all ought to have; that is, putting God in His proper place, treating God as God, the one who's the Maker of all, the Sustainer of all, our Saviour, our Sovereign, the one to whom we all need to give account.

But there's another sense of fear, and that's the sense that John means here; a fear that's linked to punishment and to terror, a fear that revolves around what God might do to us.

Some people live what they think are Christian lives, driven by that motivation and that fear. It's not true Christianity; that fear has no place in the believer's life. Look again at verse 18. 'There is no fear in love. But perfect love casts out fear, for fear has to do with punishment. And he who fears is not perfected in love.' Love and terror don't mix. They're incompatible. If terror is still there, love hasn't achieved its end; it hasn't reached its target in our lives. The whole point of God's love was to rescue us from terror. It was not designed to tell us that things didn't matter, that He would pat us on the back and say, 'There, there, it doesn't matter.' It had a design to rescue us from terror.

John describes God's love several times in his letter. He's done so earlier in this chapter, back in verses 9 and 10: 'In this the love of God was made manifest among us, that God sent his only Son into the world, so that we might live through him. In this is love, not that we love God but that he loved us and sent his Son to be the atoning sacrifice for our sins.'

When God-revealed love is described in this letter it's always in terms of the cross. It becomes clear that when John speaks of God sending His Son into the world, he's not thinking only of the incarnation but also of the redemption, not only of Christmas Day but of Good Friday. So you can't have Christmas explained to you properly unless someone talks to you about Good Friday. And God's love is no romantic gesture. It's practical and purposeful.

An uncle of mine had a golden wedding anniversary and I went up to Sheffield for it. At the end of the evening I rang home to see how things were, and I discovered that our eldest daughter was developing an ear-ache. She gets frequent infections, and the first day they're agony. I realised my wife would have to stay up most of the night with her, and would hardly get any sleep. I wanted to tell her that I really did love her, and was concerned for her. But how could I show the kind of love that's proper Christian love?

I could have said, 'Darling, I realise it will be agony for you. I'll tell you what, I do love you and, to show you, I'll try and stay up all night here as well.' Or I could have got into the car and driven back through the night and taken some of the burden off her.

If I'd been studying these verses I wouldn't have had

much choice. God didn't just send His Son so that we could have a little romantic gesture and I-love-you note. No, it's always practical and purposeful.

Look at verse 9, verse 10, verse 14. Jesus was sent to do something: to deal with sin, to take away terror. For if I have eternal life, I needn't fear eternal death, need I? If my sins have been atoned for, I needn't be terrified even of a holy God. If I'm saved, I needn't be frightened about the day of judgement.

God has set out to do all this as He reveals His love to us. 'In this is love, not that we love God but that he loved us.' It was initiative-taking love. That's why it can cast out fear.

I am not being asked to believe, you see, that we're lovely enough for God, and that therefore we can be confident for the day of judgement. None but a fool will believe that. I am not being asked to believe that if we love God enough we can have confidence for the day of judgement. When John speaks of love, and love's goal, and love's target, he's not driving me to think of my feelings for God; he's pointing me back to the cross. Now, can you look at the cross and have assurance of life, of heaven? Won't you look at the cross and get confidence for the day of judgement?

A year or so ago I went with a colleague to Westminster Chapel for a ministers' meeting before the Billy Graham '89 mission in London. We stopped for a cup of tea in their hall before the meeting started, and as we were chatting with the lady who was pouring out the tea, some-how or other the conversation started getting round to personal Christian things.

She asked me if I knew where a verse came from in the Bible, and I rather flippantly said, 'No, but that's why I always bring Helen along with me—she knows all those things!' pointing to my colleague.

Immediately the lady rounded on me and told me that it wasn't enough to have a friend who knew all the answers; I'd got to be able to answer for myself. She said, 'If you were to die tonight, and you were to face God, and He were to ask you, "Why should I let you into My heaven?", what would you say?'

She didn't have much reason to suspect me. It was a ministers' meeting I was going to—she didn't even know I was an Anglican! I've got to confess, the more I thought about that, the more I admired her. She knew that it didn't really matter what else I could offer as credentials—this is what mattered. If I could not answer that question, if I didn't have grounds for confidence on the day of judgement, then God's love hadn't reached its target in me—and it needed to.

How would you answer the same question? I'm glad I've been asked it. Can you answer confidently, without fear, or has God's love still got work to do for you?

Some of you tonight are sensitive souls who are so conscious of your sins and your shame that you'll almost refuse to believe that this confidence can be yours. And I want to say to you tonight, don't be more concerned for your sin than for God's love; don't put yourself, in the words of verse 16, outside of love; apply this love to your heart tonight, wrap it on with bandages firmly day by day. 'Abide in love,' says John; it was designed to give you confidence.

Others of you are insensitive souls. You're pretty hardened about your sins; it takes much to get you twitching. And I want to say, as we look at these verses, doesn't it remind us that there is nothing greater that God has to offer to us, than that we can be confident on the day of judgement? Our sins are infinitely more serious than we think. This is the target of God's love.

Friends, I can have thousands of genuine experiences of God, but this is His target. And if, on the other hand, all I can say is that because of Jesus I can have confidence for the day of judgement, then verse 16 tells me that that's all I need to say. And don't ever apologise for it or feel inadequate for it; God's love was targeted to do just that.

I believe it's because we've forgotten that, that we've often done much harm to the evangelical cause and the cause of evangelical unity. We so often meet in our conferences and assume the gospel, and we talk about all sorts of other things, and then we're surprised when those who want to call themselves gospel men and women start acting and speaking as if these other things are as important or more important than this.

You see, these verses tell me, there is nothing greater that God's love was designed for, than that we should have confidence on the day of judgement. I'll rejoice in that.

I can't be true to the text without adding a P.S. It's simply this:

God's love was designed to produce love

Look at verse 19: 'We love'—'*We* love because He first loved us'. We love—He expects us to be loving, says John. Of course, His great test to the true believer is whether we love or not. It has to be, if God is love, doesn't it? How can we possibly have fellowship with a God who is love and not be loving ourselves?

We love, says John, but not out of duty. The great motivation for any Christian action is not duty but gratitude. And the loving He's expecting us to be doing isn't limited to just God's love to us and our love to God; no, it's got another arm as well: it's love for one another.

That's the context in which this whole paragraph has been set.

Verse 20: 'If anyone says, "I love God," and hates his brother, he is a liar. For he who does not love his brother whom he has seen, cannot love God whom he has not seen. And this commandment we have from him, that he who loves God should love his brother also.'

Aren't they telling verses? Don't they remind us that when He urges us to abide in love, it's not just some ethereal concept? Doesn't this prick the balloon, when we want to go all super-spiritual and just think of ourselves and God?

No, the love that He's speaking about will extend to our sisters and brothers in Christ. Just look around the tent; you'll see quite a number of them, and everyone you'll see is a wicked sinner. Don't be fooled by the fact that we're all looking smart and respectable and we've got a Bible on our lap and we're at Keswick.

Now, we know those Bibles that are on our laps well enough to know that, don't we? And because we're all wicked sinners, some of us are very hard to love. But every brother or sister in Christ you see around you is also someone towards whom God has targeted that love we've been talking about, for whom Jesus died that death, so that on that day he or she can stand confidently.

So what does it mean to say, 'I love this God,' and despise a sister or brother to whom God has shown the same love I am rejoicing in?

But you'll never love the Christian family without remembering the cross. Will you remember it, day in, day out? Some of you will find it hard enough if you ever had to get close enough to me to love me, so do keep remembering the cross when you have to deal with me! And I'll ignore the insignificant Christian nonentity, if it isn't for the cross, won't I? I'll run away from the awkward Christian—if the cross doesn't draw me back.

'If anyone says, "I love God," and hates his brother, he is a liar.' You see, I can sing, 'Father, we adore You', 'Father, God, I love You', as many times as I like, but if I don't love my brother or sister Christian, God will just be saying He doesn't believe me; I'm a liar.

For God's love was designed to give me confidence on the day of judgement; God's love was designed to cast out fear; but God's love was also designed to produce love. Let's pray it does for us.

THE MARKS OF A SPIRIT-FILLED CHURCH

by Rev. Alex Ross

Acts 2

Last week I was looking at a little brochure about a church conference entitled 'Church in the Nineties'. On the programme for this conference was a man who was going to share some of the new principles that God had been teaching his church in recent years. Now, I don't know what kind of principles he's going to teach, but Christianity, in essence, is not giving us new principles today. God's final word came to us in Jesus Christ. We have all the principles we need from the apostles. We have all the principles we require in the New Testament. The challenge for us today is to rediscover the old principles, to get back to the Scriptures and see how God blessed, and how God wants us to live as Christians; to be the kind of church and people God wants us to be.

So this evening I want us to look for a little while at the marks of a Spirit-filled church. I want us to go back to the first Pentecostal church, in Acts chapter 2. We're going to try to look at the whole chapter.

Before we look through Acts 2, a couple of introductory comments.

First: Acts chapter 2 is unrepeatable. The day of Pentecost was the final saving act of Jesus Christ before His return to our planet. It's on the same level as Christmas Day, Good Friday, Easter Sunday. It cannot happen again; just as we'll never have another Christmas Day or Good Friday, so we can never have another day of Pentecost in the Acts 2 sense.

Second: Acts 2 is unreal. Everything is sweetness and light. There's great preaching; there are three thousand people saved; there's love, joy and peace in the church. It appears to be the perfect church, the kind of church we've never belonged to. But in the next four chapters we find a very different picture. We begin to see opposition from the outside, corruption on the inside, complaints and moans from the people. The apostles are nearly deflected from preaching and from prayer.

So, with those two little caveats, I want us to look at Acts chapter 2.

There's a little song that we sometimes sing: 'For I'm building a people of power'. What does it mean? Sometimes you hear people described as having 'a very powerful ministry'. What does that mean? Well, Acts 2 certainly shows us a people of power, and it certainly shows us a powerful ministry. So I'd like us to look at Acts chapter 2 under four headings; four marks of a Spirit-filled church.

1. The Holy Spirit created an interest (verses 1–4)

In the first four verses, the believers have their first experience of the Holy Spirit. The evidence of the Spirit's arrival is seen in three ways: verse 2, a violent wind; verse 3, tongues of fire; and then in verse 4, speaking in other languages.

These are not the Spirit; these are signs that the Spirit has come; a sound, a sight, a speech. But they certainly drew the crowds. Verse 6: 'When they heard this sound, a crowd came together in bewilderment, because each one heard them speaking in his own language.'

What is this phenomenon, speaking in other languages? Well, they're certainly not drunk. Paul tells us so in verse 15. Also, it's not a miracle of hearing. Look at verse 4; that makes it quite clear: 'They began to speak in other tongues as the Spirit enabled them.' And it's not incoherent language; it's not ecstatic speech that needs interpretation.

No, what we have here is a miracle, a supernatural ability to speak in the languages of all the people who are mentioned in verses 9–11. They begin to speak in Aramaic, Greek, Latin, Hebrew, Egyptian.

Notice too which people became interested (verse 5): 'Now there were staying in Jerusalem God-fearing Jews from every nation under heaven.' They're the people whom God was already at work in.

It's the same today, isn't it? Who are the people who become Christians in our church? They're normally the people who are on the fringe, who have been exposed to Christianity in some way; people who have Christian friends or family. Well, the God-fearers here were the people who saw this unusual sight, and they wanted to know more.

Life attracts life. If you walk down the High Street, people (especially men) generally walk past shop windows without a glance. But occasionally you'll see a group clustered round a window, and in that window may be a television set with the test match on, or it may be a pet shop with a dog in it, or it may be a toy shop with a train going round. But there's life in the window. That's what attracts people's attention. And so it is with a Spirit-filled church.

Of course, there's no one way. As you look around the world today you can see the Spirit of God using different churches in different ways, drawing people to Jesus Christ.

Ken T'Hoven, in his book *Breath of Heaven*, tells of the time when he was a young preacher and had been booked to lead a mission in a little Lincolnshire village. He arrived on the first night at a Methodist chapel, bright-eyed and bushy-tailed with his best sermon, and he went into the rather run-down fifty-seater chapel. The congregation was four farmers.

This went on night after night. He became very despondent. But those four farmers were meeting every day to pray. They invited him to join them, and he said later that he'd never heard men pray like it before. They wept with God, they pleaded with God, they quoted the promises of the Bible to God.

On the second Thursday of the mission he went, for some inexplicable reason, an hour early. As he approached the chapel he could see that there were bikes and tractors and cars all around the chapel. When he got inside it was so full he could hardly get to the platform. And on that night, he said, thirty-six people repented and turned to Jesus Christ, and so it continued until the end of the mission.

That is the Holy Spirit creating interest in people's lives and drawing them to Christ. It's remarkable and unusual; but this is what we want in our churches, isn't it? We want the Holy Spirit bringing people to Christ, drawing people to Christ in faith and repentance. So that's the first thing; the Holy Spirit created an interest in Jerusalem.

2. The Holy Spirit raised up a preacher (verses 14–36)

This is the largest section of the chapter, and I think it's very significant that Luke chose to give over fifty per cent of all the space he devotes to the day of Pentecost, to preaching. You may say I've got a vested interest. Well, of course I have! But it does appear that this was the thing that Luke wanted to home in on.

There must have been a lot of other things going on that day. There must have been chorus-singing, hand-clapping, counselling, even some dancing in the aisles. But the important feature that Luke highlights here is the preaching, and that's true of all revivals throughout history; preaching has played a key part.

What can we learn from Peter? What can we learn from his little sermon here? We can learn a great deal. I'd like just to note three quick things.

1. Peter preached relevantly (verses 14–21)
Notice, he started where people were; look at verse 15: 'These men are not drunk, as you suppose. It's only nine in the morning!'

You see, he was answering the question that they were asking. He didn't launch into some carefully prepared theological statement. He listened before he preached. And in each age through history there have been dominant questions that people have been asking.

In the first century there was a tremendous preoccupation with death. It baffled intellectuals, it confused philosophers, and they grappled with this whole subject. And so, when the church came along with the message of Jesus Christ, the resurrection was the spearhead of its thrust.

In the Middle Ages, there was an overriding concern with guilt: 'How do we know we can be forgiven? How do we receive forgiveness? Can we really be forgiven? Can we be put right with God?' The Reformation came along, with Martin Luther and his colleagues; the preaching of the cross and justification by faith.

What are the questions of the twentieth century? What are people asking today? If we're going to communicate relevantly with our world, we need to know those questions; we need to be listening carefully; we need to have our feet on the ground.

If you want some homework, go and look at all the

sermons in Acts. The gospel is always the same, it's always about Jesus Christ and what He's done. But they're all applied differently; they're applied relevantly to the particular situation.

Look at verses 17–21. That's very relevant, isn't it, for a crowd of Jews—quoting from Joel? The Jews used to carry Joel round in their back pocket, and so when Peter said, 'This is from Joel; Joel said this was going to happen,' they all whipped out their *Joel* and had a look to see if it was really true.

2. Peter preached Jesus (verses 22–31)
In his sermon he covers the main points of Jesus Christ: His incarnation, in verse 22 (signs and wonders); His crucifixion, verse 23 (evil man actually put Christ to death—but then that was God's plan; it was God working things out); and the main thrust, in verses 24–36, where the main space is given to the resurrection, the ascension and the exaltation of Christ (because the resurrection shows clearly who Jesus Christ is). And, of course, it was a message for the first century—we've already said that; death was on the mind of first-century men.

3. Peter preached as a witness (verses 32 and 33)
Look at verse 32: 'God has raised this Jesus to life, and we are all witnesses of the fact.'

You see, Peter had seen it all. He'd seen the signs and wonders, he'd seen Jesus die on the cross, he'd seen the resurrected Christ, he'd seen the coming Holy Spirit, and so he was preaching as a witness, as a man who not only knew but believed.

Professor Blaiklock talked about the early disciples like this:

They were men who whole-heartedly believed that Christ was God's last word to man, beyond which He would say no more. The world staggers and its skies grow dark for want of such men. That is why a vast Christian revival could still save a tottering world.

Now, of course, we can't be apostolic witnesses in this Acts 2 sense, but we do need people who not only know the Bible but believe it.

We've got a lot of Bible knowledge here tonight; we know the facts, we have a lot of knowledge. But do we actually believe what the Bible says? Do we rely on the Bible? Is our confidence in the word of God a confidence in something sharper than a two-edged sword, that actually breaks into people's lives? This is what Billy Graham says revolutionised his preaching, when he came to the conviction that what the Bible says is actually what God says, and that when the Bible speaks, God speaks.

The great eighteenth-century actor, David Garrick, was once asked by a church leader how he produced such wonderful effects on his listeners when reciting fiction. Garrick said, 'Because I recite fiction as if it were truth, and you preach truth as if it were fiction.' That could be the twentieth-century church, couldn't it? So often we're apologetic, we water it down; so often we keep our mouths closed when we should be speaking out. You see, you don't have to stand in front of hundreds of people; it's not that dramatic. But we do need people like Peter, who are prepared to stand as witnesses for Christ in our world.

A friend of mine died a couple of weeks ago, and as he was going on the way to the hospital—he had had a brain haemorrhage—he was staring at the tattoo on the ambulance man's arm.

The ambulance man said to him, 'What is it you're looking at?'

So he said, 'Well, I'm looking at the cross and the flowers on your arm.'

'Yes,' said the ambulance man. 'When my mother died

I was unable to get to the funeral, so I put this cross and the flowers on as a memory for her.'

My friend said, 'I know a man who died on a cross.'

And the ambulance man said, 'Well, tell me about Him.'

So my friend just talked quite clearly about Jesus Christ and how He died on the cross for the world, to that ambulance man.

It doesn't need to be anything big. You can do it lying on your back, wherever you are. But we do need people who will speak the gospel message directly and clearly.

Look at verse 40: 'With many other words he warned them; and he pleaded with them, "Save yourselves from this corrupt generation." '

When did we last plead with anyone? When did we actually warn anyone, 'Look, you must save yourself from this corrupt world'? That's the kind of man Peter was.

So the Holy Spirit raised up a preacher.

3. The Holy Spirit brought a response (verses 37–39)

When the people heard this, they were cut to the heart and said to Peter and the other apostles, 'Brothers, what shall we do?' (verse 37). That's a question we'd love to hear, isn't it, when we're talking to our pagan friends!

We can't create a response like that. Only the Holy Spirit can cut people to the heart and cause them to ask such questions. We can preach our heads off till we're blue in the face, and it can just be like bouncing off a brick wall. Only the Holy Spirit can bring conviction. And that's what's happening here.

William Grimshaw, the famous eighteenth-century preacher, was rector of Hawarth. When he was appointed to the church it was dead. On Sunday about twelve people, out of the village population of 2,600, turned up for church. There hadn't been a minister there for twenty-one years. It's reckoned that in the village there was more beer consumed than water.

But Grimshaw began to preach and the church began to fill up. In fact, people used to have to stand outside to hear him preaching. Men were seized with weeping as he told the gospel story. People used to come into Hawarth from the countryside around, crying out in pain with the fear of sin and God's wrath.

That's the convicting power of the Holy Spirit! You see, we can't do that ourselves. Only God can bring about that kind of response. And we don't see too much of that in our churches. We haven't had too many people crying out in our church recently, not too many people weeping under the wrath of God.

In verse 41 we see that three thousand people got up out of their seats and went forward. Jesus never saw anything like that in His whole ministry. Oh, yes, He fed lots of people; but He never saw people repent and believe on this scale. That's the work of the Holy Spirit.

I notice here, also, that the Holy Spirit breaks down the barriers. Verse 39: 'The promise is for you and your children and for all who are far off.' That's us in Keswick. The Holy Spirit is for us here, because we're far off from Jerusalem in the first century.

Go back to verse 17: ' "In the last days," God says, "I will pour out my Spirit on all people. Your sons and daughters will prophesy, your young men will see visions, your old men will dream dreams. Even on my servants, both men and women, I will pour out my Spirit in those days." '

The barriers are broken down. Barriers of sex—men and women; barriers of age—young and old; barriers of rank—'even on my servants'.

In our churches there's a terrific amount of activity, an awful lot of action. We have all our programmes. But what is the response of the world? Is there conviction? Are people turning in repentance?

If the Holy Spirit were taken away it's reckoned that an awful lot of our activity would go on regardless. But the Holy Spirit in Acts 2 created a response of repentance and faith.

4. The Holy Spirit created a community (verses 42–47)

When the three thousand went forward, in verse 41, it was only the beginning. As it's said; our salvation is free, but it will cost us everything we've got.

We begin to see here in Acts 2 how the Holy Spirit begins to create a new community. If you want a vision of your local church, if you've become a little bit jaundiced with the church fellowship you belong to, it's a marvellous vision here in Acts 2.

Four qualities of the new church:

1. They were a learning church (verse 42)

They devoted themselves to the apostles' teaching and to the fellowship, to the breaking of bread and to prayer.

The Holy Spirit on that day opened a new school in Jerusalem, and there were three thousand in the kindergarten right from the word 'go'. This is the first Christian basics that any church ever had.

2. They were a loving church (verses 44–46)

They met together daily, they shared together, they ate together; they knew what was going on in one another's lives. Very often in our own churches these days, we just meet at the porch and we really have no idea of what's going on in our lives.

A little while ago we had a family who'd been away in America and they'd gone to visit Disney World. One of the children had brought back a stuffed animal, Dumbo, and she brought it to church on the first Sunday that she was back. On the way out the mother was coming out through the church door, and there was a man by her side whom I'd never seen before. She said to me, 'Have you met Dumbo yet?' So I said, 'No, I haven't'—and shook hands with the man. He said he was a lawyer and was going to sue me...

But that's the kind of church fellowship that we often live in today. We're very remote; we're very busy; life is very fast; and we're not really sharing together and eating together and getting to know one another; there isn't much of a community in our society. Communities are, by and large, gone, certainly in the towns and the cities. And in the churches, we need a community like this.

3. They were a worshipping church (verses 46–47)
They continued in the temple but they also met in their homes. Notice that they would have had formal worship and informal worship. Notice also that in those verses there is awe and there is joy; they're not mutually exclusive; they go together.

4. They were an evangelistic church (verse 47)

> ...praising God and enjoying the favour of all the people. And the Lord added to their number daily those who were being saved.

These early Christians were not so preoccupied with their learning and their loving and their worshipping that they forgot the people outside. The church in the book of Acts is always a missionary church, an evangelistic church. And we see here that it wasn't just a special time of mission; people were being added daily. They just didn't invite Billy Graham over for a week to do mission. It was happening daily: it was part of their life-style.

So four things we learn; four marks of the Spirit-filled church: it was a church that created an interest; it was a church that took preaching seriously; it was a church that actually saw a response, conviction; it was a church that loved and learned and worshipped and evangelised.

If I'm honest, reading Acts 2 has made me rather dissatisfied with my own life, as I've studied the chapter and as I've seen this first Pentecostal church. It's made me tired of the poverty of my own Christian life. It's made me dissatisfied, too, with my home church. I long to see us far more like Acts 2!

I know Acts 2 is unrepeatable; I know Acts 2 in many ways is unreal; but it does show us the church at its best. In so many ways we become satisfied with second-best. So it's a challenge to us as individuals, and to our churches.

KESWICK 1990 TAPES AND VIDEOS

Tapes
Here is a list of tape numbers for each of the addresses included in this volume, in the order in which they appear.

The Bible Readings
Bishop Michael Baughen: KA1/90,   KA2/90,   KA3/90, KA4/90
Mr Charles Price: KB31/90, KB32/90, KB33/90, KB34/90

The Addresses

Dr Warren Wiersbe	KA7/90
Rev. Ian Barclay	KA8/90
Mr Billy Strachan	KA10/90
Rev. Michael Wilcock	KB37/90
Rev. Hugh Palmer	KB38/90
Rev. Alex Ross	KB40/90
Rev. Philip Hacking	KA9/90

To order, send your remittance (£2.95 sterling, plus 45p p&p per cassette), to:

> International Christian Communications
> Silverdale Road
> Eastbourne
> Sussex BN20 7AB.

A catalogue of other Keswick tapes available may be obtained from the same address.

Videos
All the addresses in this book are also available on VHS video. To order, send your remittance (£22.45 sterling, inc. p&p, for each set of four Bible Readings; £9.95 for individual videos, plus £2.50 p&p) to:

Bagster Video
PO Box 700
Alton
Hants
GU34 1EN

If posted in the U.K. no stamp is needed; instead mark the envelope *FREEPOST*. Details of other Keswick videos may be obtained from the same address.

KESWICK 1991

The annual Keswick Convention takes place each July at the heart of England's beautiful Lake District. The two separate weeks of the Convention offer an unparalleled opportunity for listening to gifted Bible exposition, experiencing Christian fellowship with believers from all over the world, and enjoying something of the unspoilt grandeur of God's creation.

Each of the two weeks has a series of four morning Bible Readings, followed by other addresses throughout the rest of the day. The programme in the second week is a little less intensive, and it is often referred to as 'Holiday Week'. There are also regular meetings throughout the fortnight for young people, and in the second week for children.

The dates for the 1991 Keswick Convention are 13–20 July (Convention Week) and 20–27 July (Holiday Convention Week). The Bible Reading speakers are Dr R. T. Kendall and Rev. Roy Clements. Other speakers during the fortnight are Dr Luis Palau, Rev. John Balchin, Rev. Alistair Begg, Rev. David Coffey, Rev. David Cohen, Rev. Liam Goligher and Rev. David Jackman.

Further details may be obtained from:

The Keswick Convention Secretary
PO Box 292
Harrow
Middlesex
HA1 2NP
England